GW00320208

PSYCHO-SELLING

PSYCHO-SELLING

DOUBLE YOUR INCOME FROM SALES IN EIGHT WEEKS

BRUCE KING

BBC BOOKS

Dedicated to all salespeople
without whom all commerce would cease.
Don't ever think of quitting –
the only losers are the quitters.
And to
Gemma and Natasha
I'm sorry I couldn't come out to play.

Published by BBC Books,
a division of BBC Enterprises Limited,
Woodlands, 80 Wood Lane
London W12 0TT

First published 1994
© Bruce King 1994
ISBN 0 563 36770 9

Designed by Tim Higgins
Set in Linotype Palatino by Phoenix Photosetting Ltd, Chatham, Kent
Printed and bound in Great Britain by Redwood Books, Trowbridge
Jacket printed by Lawrence Allen Ltd, Weston-super-Mare

CONTENTS

FOREWORD   7

PREFACE   9

HOW TO USE THIS BOOK   12

WEEK ONE
PSYCHO-DYNAMIC PROGRAMMING –
TO MAKE YOU THE BEST   18

WEEK TWO
PSYCHO-SELLING TECHNIQUES –
VITAL KEYS TO SALES SUCCESS   25

WEEK THREE
BUYERS AND THEIR PSYCHOLOGICAL PROFILES 39
PSYCHO-SELLING TECHNIQUES THAT MAKE THEM
WANT TO BUY

WEEK FOUR
PERFECT PROSPECTS
HOW TO IDENTIFY THEM AND MAKE THEM COME TO YOU 53

WEEK FIVE
PSYCHO-SELLING TELEPHONE TECHNIQUES
AND PRESENTATIONS   70

WEEK SIX
THE PSYCHOLOGY BEHIND OBJECTIONS AND
HOW TO DEAL WITH THEM   89

WEEK SEVEN
CLOSE THAT SALE   107
PSYCHO-CLOSES THAT GUARANTEE SALES SUCCESS

WEEK EIGHT
YOU HAVE THE POWER!   132

SUMMARY   141

APPENDIX
RECORD KEEPING   142

FOREWORD

Psycho: Indicating the mind or psychological or mental processes.
Selling: To promote the sale of, to gain acceptance of.
Collins New English Dictionary, 2nd edition, 1986

Psycho-Selling: Using your brain to get someone else's brain to want to buy what you have to sell.
Bruce King

The top 5 per cent of salespeople are among the highest paid individuals in the world today. Of those top 5 per cent, only a few will have any knowledge of some of the techniques taught in this book. Some will have stumbled on them by accident and will not even be aware that they are using them. Others will have learnt one or two from one of the few brilliant salespeople who are prepared to share some of the secrets of their amazing success.

This book represents a radical deviation from the style and content of most books that claim to improve your sales performance. In the chapters that follow, you will learn techniques to take you right to the top of what is one of the oldest, boldest and most lucrative forms of employment available today.

There is another definition of Psycho: 'madness'.

Frankly, you would have to be mad not to buy this book and put these techniques to the test. I know that they work and I know that, by applying the lessons taught in this book, you can double your income in just eight weeks. Not only that, but you will also enjoy your work a lot more – and have a lot more fun.

PREFACE

I have spent the last twenty-five years selling all kinds of products and ideas to all kinds of people and teaching others to do the same. I have probably earned more money than most other salespeople in the United Kingdom and each year my income goes up by leaps and bounds. This has not happened by accident.

As a former student of psychology, I have always been fascinated by the mental processes involved when people make decisions. When I first embarked on my selling career, I set out to investigate and fine tune these processes so that nobody I was ever trying to sell to would ever say 'no' to me. They don't any more. Let's face it – you bought this book just because of the message on the very first page.

It has taken me years to develop and perfect my techniques and involved me in hundreds of hours of study – and hundreds more practising and perfecting my ideas. However, it isn't going to take you that long. The years of practice, and my eagerness to pass this knowledge on to other people, also led me to simplify my ideas so that they could be taught in the shortest possible time and with maximum effectiveness. You may never earn quite as much as I do but, by following my instructions, you are certainly going to be in a position where, within eight weeks, you can earn twice as much as you have ever earned before.

How do I know this? It's quite simple. Hundreds of people have already dramatically increased their incomes beyond their wildest imagination as a result of learning these new skills. I taught the 'Clenched Fist' technique in Week Eight to a computer salesman while sharing a cab for fifteen minutes on a wet Thursday afternoon. He called me the following morning to tell me he had signed a contract with his client that had earned him more on that one sale than he had earned in the previous seven months. During our drive he had told me that he felt his chances of closing that sale were one in a thousand. By the time our journey had ended, I had known there was only one chance in a thousand that he wouldn't close it.

I taught the same technique to a group of eight life insurance salespeople in a half-hour session. During the following week, seven of them earned twice as much as in any other week in the previous six months.

A little while ago I received a letter from a saleswoman who had been on one of my weekend training seminars the previous year. At the time she attended, she was unable to meet the sales targets set for her by her company and was thinking of leaving her job and going back to college. The letter contained a photograph of her standing beside her brand-new sports car, a gift from the company. Not only had she sold twice as much as the runner-up in the firm's sales competition, but she had also been offered a promotion to sales manager. She declined. She was already earning much more than the sales manager's boss.

These are just a few examples of how learning the techniques of Psycho-Selling have worked for other people – and how they can work for you.

Let me give you an example of how psychology can work both for and against you in sales.

Richard is a top salesman with a large agricultural-machinery manufacturer. He attended my seminar because, in his own words, 'I want to be even better than I am now'. During one of the breaks he told me how his business had failed, how he had been on the point of giving up on life and how, ten years previously, in a last desperate effort, he had applied for a sales job with an office equipment company.

As with so many people when they are first recruited into the sales profession, his prospective employer had sold him the job. Let's face it, when a company pays a very low salary, if any at all, and when your income is dependent on you getting out there and selling, they don't have a great deal to lose if they make the wrong choice. Richard was told that the job was easy, that he would make a fortune, that anyone could do it and that little training was necessary. He took it and, after four days learning about the products he was to sell, off he went into the big wide world. All the enthusiasm engendered during those first few days rubbed off on him. Psychology at work. After the first week on the road, he returned to the office with a bundle of order forms for various items of equipment. He felt good about himself for the first time in ages. Life was good again – or was it? Back at the office he met some of his sales colleagues and that was when psychology turned against him.

'You've been lucky this week,' one said.

'Your first week is always good and after that it's downhill all the way,' another said.

'The competition's too stiff'.

And guess what? Correct. At the end of the second week, he had sold nothing.

Fortunately for Richard, he never forgot the excitement of that first week, or the money he had made. He vowed to make a success of himself. He studied his product range, he went to various sales training courses to improve his sales techniques and he studied avariciously. He has never looked back. Yet that very first encounter with what psychology can do could have been the final nail in his coffin.

Before I go on to explain how to use this book, let me emphasize that, although I am going to teach you how to use Psycho-Selling to increase your sales dramatically, these techniques are not a substitute for a poor technical knowledge of your product or service. If you don't know enough about what you are trying to sell, you had better find out fast.

I have often heard sales managers tell their salespeople that technical knowledge is not important; that as long as they know 5 per cent more than the person they are selling to they will appear to be experts. Make no mistake about that statement – it's rubbish. If you really want the fortune that being a top salesperson can bring, it is essential to know the technical aspects of the product or service you are selling. Why? First of all, the average customer is a lot more informed than he or she might have been some years ago. They are looking for expert advice and, in this highly competitive world, it is readily available to them. Second, and even more important, in order to maximize the benefits available from Psycho-Selling you are going to have to believe that you are the very best there is. You may be able to fool a few customers but you can't fool yourself. If you don't know what you're selling, how can you expect anyone to buy it.

HOW TO USE
THIS BOOK

Most books on the techniques of selling tend to concentrate almost entirely on prospecting for new clients, presentation skills and closing the sale. I have nothing against that approach except that, for most people, it doesn't achieve significant results.

I too will be covering those same topics in later chapters, and in a lot of detail. The difference is that by the time you get on to them, the techniques you have learned beforehand will increase the effectiveness of what you will learn several fold.

During your induction into the techniques of Psycho-Selling I am going to ask you to do various things that you may not be used to doing. The main reason is that you and I are both in a hurry. You are in a hurry to double your income in the next eight weeks and I am eager to help you make it happen. I am therefore going to ask you to accept without question certain statements that I make.

I know that, under normal circumstances, it is every person's right to demand evidence before accepting anything. However, how many times during any normal working day do you take things at face value without question? Your train in the morning may not really be going to its stated destination. The person sitting next to you may look and act like a city businessman but could be out of work, a confidence trickster or a plumber; his appearance normally leads you to make an assumption without thinking. Most people accept what they read in their daily paper as the truth – yet how many times have you heard that you shouldn't believe everything you read in the newspapers. Let's be honest. We do what suits us.

The explanations for what I am going to ask you to do **are** available. However, to document them to your total satisfaction could occupy an entire shelf in even the largest library. The techniques of Psycho-Selling are distilled from research by some of the world's greatest psychologists and many of its most successful salespeople. To ask you to read and digest this research to satisfy your curiosity and justify your involvement would defeat the object of the exercise.

I ask only that you give me an hour of your time every day and practise the lessons you will learn. The end will most definitely justify the means. When I have finished writing this book I shall be out teaching people to sell and be selling myself.

In eight weeks time, you should be earning at least double your current income. Give us both a chance!

The human brain is extremely complex but, for the sake of simplicity, let us divide it into just two parts. I shall refer to them as the 'conscious mind' and the 'subconscious mind'. This is probably not a new concept to anybody.

The conscious mind is the one you are in control of. It is the analytical part of the brain that talks to you in words all the time. It is the one you hear very clearly in your head whenever you think.

The subconscious mind is the part that very few people ever listen to regularly but, in truth, it controls many of your decision-making processes and the way you react to people and different situations. Everyone has experienced a 'gut feeling'. That's the subconscious mind. It is rarely wrong because its knowledge is based on millions of experiences that you are unable to remember with your conscious mind.

The first important point I want you to accept is that real learning can only take place when your mind is at least somewhere between the conscious and the subconscious stage. It is only when you take in information in this state that the subconscious mind will allow you to use its knowledge when you really need to, without the conscious mind fighting it.

Accept, then, that you cannot fully learn the techniques of Psycho-Selling by quickly reading a chapter going to work on the train, in a short break between sales calls, while grabbing a hurried meal or, in fact, at any time when your mind is not fully capable of absorbing the information you need. Therefore, for just a few weeks, accept this simple discipline: read only one of the following chapters a week and practise what you have learned during the week in conjunction with the simple exercises I will teach you. I accept, of course, that you will have a quick flip through the following pages to get an overview of what you have just invested in but, after that, if you seriously want to double your income in the next few weeks, you must follow my instructions.

The second important point that you must accept without question is that nothing can ever happen until you know what you want to happen.

That is quite a radical statement – or is it? If I had said that you can't find the way to a particular place until you decide what place you want to go to, it would have made absolute sense. Accept, therefore, that your life cannot change until you decide how you would like it to be.

You must also accept that the fastest way to make things happen is to make sure that your subconscious mind, as well as your conscious mind, knows clearly what it is you want to happen – and that the fastest way to get this message through to the subconscious mind is to visualize exactly what it is you want. Once you have put a clear mental picture into your subconscious mind there is no need to worry any longer about how things will happen. Just accept that they most definitely will. This technique is known as Psycho-Dynamic Programming and will be expanded upon in later chapters. For the moment, I will illustrate this by way of an example.

Some years ago, I was involved in teaching people to walk barefoot across beds of burning hot coals. The reason for these 'Fire-Walking Seminars' was to demonstrate that it is possible to achieve the seemingly impossible in a very short period of time. The training consisted of a short period of deep relaxation, just like the exercise you will practise later, followed by ten minutes of visualizing walking across the coals. More than fifty people were taught this simple visualization technique at each one of our seminars and at the end of the training very few lacked the confidence to walk across the burning coals. With few exceptions, there was not a blister in sight. Visualization is the key to programming the subconscious mind, and one of the keys to helping you to achieve what you want from life.

At the end of the book there is a chart which you will start during the next chapter. At the end of each week you will monitor the improvement in your sales performance. If those sales figures are not increasing every week over the next eight weeks there can be only one of two reasons: either you are not following my instructions or you are just not going to work.

I expect you to read each chapter twice during the week. Before doing so, carry out the following exercise and repeat this exercise daily together with others described in some of the chapters.

Try this first exercise when you have finished this chapter and then read these first pages again. You will immediately notice how much more easily you absorb the information. What's more, tomorrow it will be as fresh in your mind as if you had just read it.

Just one more word before you start. Let us not confuse the techniques you will learn with brainwashing. Brainwashing is something that is forced upon you. You volunteered to double your income. Having said that, I can think of a lot of good reasons for people having their brains washed once in a while to get rid of some of those cobwebs that have been holding them back from the success they deserve.

YOUR DAILY EXERCISES

First, make absolutely certain that you are not going to be disturbed for the next half an hour. Take the telephone off the hook or switch on your answering machine if you have one. If there is anybody in the house or office, or wherever you intend to carry out these exercises, make sure they understand your absolute need for privacy. After all, it is likely to be in their best interests as well as yours.

Now sit in a comfortable chair, make sure you can see your watch or a clock easily, read the rest of these instructions and then just put them into practice.

Relaxation

I want you to close your eyes and take several deep breaths in and out. I then want you to concentrate on relaxing and letting the tension go from every part of your body. Start with your toes and go up your legs, bit by bit, until you have reached and relaxed your buttocks. Then do the same with your arms, starting with your fingers and working up until you end with your shoulders fully relaxed. All this time, I would like you to breathe steadily and gently. When your shoulders are fully relaxed, start at the top of your head – your scalp – and work down the back of your neck and your back to your waist. Next, make sure your forehead is relaxed, then all the muscles of your face, particularly your jaw. Finally, allow your chest muscles to relax. This whole process should take no more than five minutes.

For the next fifteen minutes I want you to do absolutely nothing but concentrate on the sound of your breathing. Please realize that it is inevitable that from time to time you will find that your mind is drifting in all different directions. That's fine. All you need do when you realize this is happening is go back to concentrating on your breathing. Remember that you do this for a full fifteen minutes. If you need to check your watch or the clock, only open one eye. This keeps the sub-conscious mind focused.

Visualization

At the end of this relaxation exercise I want you to sit there for another ten minutes, still with your eyes closed, and do nothing but visualize all the wonderful things you are going to be able to do when you have doubled your income. This is very serious. Whatever it is that you can buy and enjoy, picture it clearly and in detail.

Read these instructions one more time so that you fully understand them, then put them into practice. I'll see you later in Week One.

Summary of Key Points

● Read only one chapter a week and read each chapter twice during the week. Practise your exercises every day.

● Real learning only takes place when the mind is somewhere between the conscious and subconscious stage.

● Nothing can ever happen until you know what it is you want to happen.

● The fastest way to make things happen is to put a clear picture into your subconscious mind of what it is you want to happen. The subconscious mind will then make it happen for you. This process is known as Psycho-Dynamic Programming.

WEEK ONE

PSYCHO-DYNAMIC PROGRAMMING – TO MAKE YOU THE BEST

It's a common saying that 'the easiest person to sell to is a salesman'. That statement is absolutely correct. Over the years I have bought every imaginable high-tech and low-tech gizmo, gadget and adult toy that has been foisted on me by an enthusiastic salesperson. I have bought brand-new cars when all I needed was a change of tyres, new suits when all I needed was a button sewn on a jacket and services from a variety of consultants, merely because they convinced me that I would be better off as a result.

The common factor in every case was that the person selling to me was an expert. I knew exactly what he or she was doing, what sales techniques they were using and what hot buttons they were pressing. Why did I buy? Very simply – they made me want to.

When I am being sold something by a very good salesperson, I really can't help myself. I enjoy being part of the sale. I thrive on the salesperson's enthusiasm and I never regret a purchase. In fact, I probably enjoy whatever it is that I bought even more.

The moral to this story is simple. If someone who knows all the tricks of the trade can be sold to so easily, imagine how easy it is to sell to someone who knows none of them.

Now let me tell you why selling is the only profession in which you can make a fortune. And I mean a fortune. There are basically two types of salespeople, those who serve – they don't really sell at all – and those who are paid to sell. The servers of the world usually work on a basic salary and maybe, in a good month, collect a small bonus.

Real money is made by salespeople who work in competitive environments and who, generally speaking, are paid a low basic salary and very high commission rates. The really interesting point is that commissions are as a rule pitched at a level that will provide the average salesperson with an average income. Bear in mind that 80 per cent of all sales are made by 20 per cent of the salespeople, and that 80 per cent of that 80 per cent are made by the top 10 per cent of the 20 per cent, and you can see why so many top salespeople are millionaires.

I promised that you could double your income in just eight weeks. You could also be one of those millionaires – all you have to do is become one of the very best at what you do. This chapter is going to make sure it happens.

Before we go any further, I would like you to start the sales progress monitor chart at the end of the book. Assuming that you can double your income by doubling your sales over the next eight weeks, all you have to do is increase your sales by 10 per cent each week and you will reach your target figure.

To check your progress, select your very best eight-consecutive-week sales period and enter your sales figures in the relevant columns. Then, at the end of each week, enter your figures for that week. You will be amazed at the differences.

I am assuming that you have by now brushed up on the technical knowledge you need to sell your product and that you are raring to go. Are you the best? You probably don't think so. Well, if you don't nobody else is going to think so either.

BE ENTHUSIASTIC – BE CARING – BE THE BEST THERE IS

How many times have you gone out with the intention of buying something and walked out of a shop or store because the salesperson was unenthusiastic and boring? I have, many times. The price of the product was almost immaterial. I wanted someone to be as enthusiastic as I was about what I wanted to buy. Sometimes the salesperson has been so unenthusiastic that he or she has even put me off buying the product from anybody at all. Other times, I have paid 50 per cent more than I need have done elsewhere, just because the person selling it was a great salesperson and even more enthusiastic than I was.

People love to buy from the very best and the very enthusiastic. They also love to buy from people who care – about their customers and their products.

A few years ago I was driving past a car showroom and noticed a brand-new, and very expensive, convertible sports car inside. With the hood down, it looked absolutely magnificent. Let me make it very clear that at the time I was most definitely not in the market for a new car, let alone one with that kind of price tag.

Nevertheless, purely out of interest, I parked my car and strolled into the showroom, just to take a closer look at this beautifully polished, white and chrome, dream on wheels.

You guessed it. I bought it. Or rather – I was sold it. That salesman was one of the best I've come across in a long time, and he knew it. But, because he knew it, he really didn't come across as a salesman. Was he confident? Absolutely. There was no sign of nerves. He gave me a very friendly and polite smile and demonstrated an eagerness to show off his product. He wasn't in the slightest bit intimidated by me or the fact that if he didn't sell me the car he would lose a very large commission.

He didn't pounce on me and make me feel that I was being lined up to pay for his next holiday in the Bahamas. He was just confident, friendly and very eager to help.

Did he care about his product? I've never seen anyone care as much as this man did! He was immaculately dressed and carrying a very clean and nearly new yellow duster. He noticed several invisible finger-marks on that gleaming paintwork and delicately and lovingly polished them away while gently easing me into a conversation. He dusted tiny specks from the upholstery before I was asked to sit in the driver's seat. He gently wiped the leather steering-wheel before I got in, and polished the tiniest smear from the windscreen as I settled behind the wheel. All this was done quietly, discreetly and with absolutely genuine care for his product.

Did he care about me? You bet he did! He helped me off with my jacket so that it wouldn't crease when I sat in the driver's seat. He removed the price ticket from the windscreen so that I could get a perfect view of how that long, gleaming bonnet would look when I was driving it.

He adjusted the seat for me, explained the controls quietly and with no hint of impatience and, when I was finally sitting comfortably admiring the deep-pile carpets and the magnificent dashboard, he told me how well I looked in the car, with the perfect choice of words.

Was he enthusiastic? It goes without saying. There wasn't a question he didn't answer as if it was more important to him than it was to me. He never criticized his competition. He only emphasized how much more I would love driving this car than any other, how I would be thrilled with its road-holding and comfort, how I would be delighted with its economical fuel consumption and how proud his company would be to look after the car for me when it needed any attention.

He also informed me that, by some amazing coincidence, a client of his was looking for the very car I was driving at the time and that he could therefore quote me a much better trade-in price for it. Of course, I never queried what the normal quote would have been. We had coffee in a quiet corner of the showroom and discussed the financing package but, by this time, it was merely a formality. I had been sold the car an hour ago and, even though I couldn't really afford it, I had to have it – and knew that with a little bit of extra sales effort on my part the purchase would not really cause me any financial problems.

I still have that car today, and some of the techniques I learned from that salesman have paid for it many, many times over.

So how are we going to get you to be the best, the most enthusiastic, the most caring about your product and your client in the next seven days? Very simply. By using Psycho-Dynamic Programming.

PSYCHO-DYNAMIC EXERCISES

From now on, every morning before leaving home or when you are sitting quietly in your car or office before you start work, just take a few deep breaths and carry out the relaxation exercise on page 15. After this twenty-minute period, I want you to carry out the visualization exercise on page 15: for ten minutes, imagine again all the things you would like to do, all the objects you would like to acquire and all the places you would like to visit. If you don't have the time to do these exercises first thing in the morning, do them any time you wish before you get home in the evening.

Every night, when you get home, practise the relaxation exercise for the full twenty minutes. When that time is up, I want you to repeat the

21

statement below over and over again for a full ten minutes. Don't speak it aloud. Repeat it silently to yourself, over and over again. All manner of thoughts may enter your mind and the occasional negative one may even take over. The cardinal rule is quite simple. Whenever you become aware that you are no longer concentrating on repeating the statement, return immediately to doing so. Everything will work as it should. There is no need to make up for lost time, no need for concern – and no reason to doubt that the techniques of Psycho-Dynamic Programming will work for you as they have worked for thousands of other salespeople.

Before you start, and especially if these techniques appear to be too simple, let me remind you that it is the simplest ideas that have made the greatest fortunes. The techniques of Psycho-Dynamic Programming go back many centuries. They have been practised in many forms by many different and great civilizations. Only now, for the first time in many years, is the interest in these brilliant and obvious sciences being revived. The statement you will make is as follows:

> *I (your name), am the greatest of all salespeople.*
> *I am so enthusiastic about what I do, I love what*
> *I sell and I care passionately about my products and*
> *my customers.*
> (Repeat over and over for ten minutes)

PSYCHO-DYNAMIC LABELLING

Following these instructions is not quite enough. To benefit totally from Psycho-Dynamic Programming the subconscious mind needs constant reminders of the role it is expected to fulfil on your behalf. You are therefore going to have to remind it throughout the day.

I am sure there are hundreds of examples of notices that you pass every day that you do not really see but which you act upon. Let me quote a few: 'Turn Left', 'No Right Turn', 'No Entry', 'Keep Off the Grass', etc. You see them, but you don't really see them. You act on their instructions, but it is almost always your subconscious mind that gives them to your conscious mind.

Let's try another simple example. You are walking towards a puddle while engaged in a deep conversation with a friend. You don't say to yourself, 'There is a puddle, I must walk around it or my shoes, socks and, possibly, my feet will get wet.' What actually happens is that your conscious mind sees the puddle but, because you are concentrating on your conversation, your subconscious mind overrides it and reminds it that certain actions are necessary if it doesn't want a rude surprise.

Your plan, therefore, must be to place constant reminders in front of your subconscious mind all day long. Acquire about twenty-five small, self-adhesive labels. On some of them write 'I am the very, very best'. On others write 'I am wildly enthusiastic about what I do'. On the remainder write 'I love my products and my clients'.

If any of these phrases irritate you, or their wording is not quite as you would like it to be, change them to whatever you prefer as long as the sense remains the same. When you have completed this, I want you to stick the labels on places you will frequently come across during the course of the day. Your bathroom mirror, the rear mirror and speedometer in your car, the front of your diary or appointment schedule, your watch strap and the calendar on your desk are just a few examples.

After the first day, your conscious mind will hardly notice the phrases, but your subconscious mind will see them every time you so much as glance in their direction. Their message will be constantly reinforced, possibly several hundred times a day, and you will hardly notice it happening. By the end of the first week you will be well on your way to being among the very best, most enthusiastic and caring salespeople there are.

How about a little extra income this week? Possibly even a lot. Here is what you do in conjunction with the above to achieve it. Before every sales presentation that you make this week, whether it's prospecting for a client or a face-to-face selling appointment, before you pick up the telephone or walk into the meeting just pump yourself up. With a big smile on your face and a puffed-out chest, repeat ten times:

I'm the best. I'm the very best salesperson there is. The sale is mine for the taking.

You will be astonished at the results and I shall be equally amazed if, by the end of this first week, you are not already ahead of our target.

Summary of Key Points

● The technical aspects of your product or service are assumed to be familiar to you.

● People love to buy from the best salespeople.

● The best salespeople know they are the best. They are confident, enthusiastic, friendly, care about their products and care about their customers.

● Practise your exercises every morning and evening – this will make you confident, enthusiastic and caring.

● Attach self-adhesive message labels where they will constantly be seen and registered by your subconscious mind.

● Before every sales presentation, whether over the telephone or face to face, repeat ten times to yourself: *'I'm the best. I'm the very best salesperson there is. The sale is mine for the asking'*.

● Enter your sales figures at the end of the week on your progress monitor chart.

WEEK TWO

PSYCHO-SELLING TECHNIQUES – VITAL KEYS TO SALES SUCCESS

The days of the travelling snake oil salesman are over. In today's sophisticated and competitive market-place there is no room for the slick, sly, take the money and run salesperson. In fact, let's be honest, there is nowhere to run to.

Buyers are so much more aware than in the past of what is available to them, and from whom, that to earn your fortune you have to provide them with exactly what they want. The real money today is made by salespeople who are able to make people want the product or service they have to offer, even when someone had not previously wanted it.

THE PRINCIPLE OF WIN-WIN

There is one fundamental principle that should dominate everything you do in your sales career if you really want to be among the top 5 per cent of salespeople and earn the fortune that can be earned. This is known as 'Win-Win'.

The principle of Win-Win is one that is ignored by almost all salespeople. Yet, if you adopt it, this alone could double your income. Win-Win means quite simply that unless both the seller and the buyer benefit from the transaction, the sale is most unlikely to go ahead. Even if it did, and the salesperson was the only winner, the chances of repeat business with that customer would be negligible; and the possibility of being referred to his or her friends, colleagues or business associates would be zero.

If, on the other hand, the buyer was the only winner, the salesperson, who had earned nothing on the transaction, would hardly be likely to want to repeat that same exercise again no matter how many referred leads he or she was given.

Real money can therefore only be earned when both buyer and seller are willing and excited participants in the sales process, and when both gain from doing business with each other.

Take our snake oil salesman as an example. In his day, the country was much bigger than it is today. Communication was poor – and almost non-existent between some areas. He merely had to travel from town to town and keep moving to avoid being caught. Woe betide him if he didn't keep his records properly and went back to the same town by mistake. Many a snake oil salesman did, and many were found hanging by the neck from an old yew tree or were tarred and feathered and run out of town.

What is our modern-day equivalent of snake oil? It is any product that does not do for the buyer what it says it will do; any product that relies on a follow-up service which is not provided; or any service that does not provide the results that were promised.

Those definitions cover a lot of products or services that you could be involved with.

If you are selling hair restorer that does not restore hair, glue that does not stick, insurance that does not pay out, computers that do not compute, cars that break down or, in fact, any product that does not do what you say it will do, you should not be selling it.

The choice of products and services that need selling is so vast that there is no need for you to be involved with anything that does not work and does not benefit the customer.

If you are selling a product that relies on an after-sales service that has to be provided either by yourself or by other employees within a company, you had better make sure that it delivers what it promises. Nobody wants a photocopier that cannot be regularly maintained, a car or any piece of mechanical equipment that cannot be serviced quickly and efficiently by the supplier, a software programme that cannot be modified when necessary or, in fact, anything that cannot fulfil the functions it was intended to fulfil.

If you are operating in a totally service-based industry, service is precisely what your company should be providing. If it isn't, either change the way the company is operating or change your job.

The easiest way to adapt to the principle of Win-Win is to forget completely what's in it for you and concentrate entirely on how best you can cater for your clients' or customers' needs. Never, never, sell anything to anybody on the basis of what you are going to earn if you make a sale. Only ever consider why and how your customer will benefit. If you carry this thought with you, and structure all your sales presentations accordingly, your customers will know subconsciously that you are acting in their best interests and will want to do business with you. The opposite also applies. If you are only thinking about what the sale will do for you, the customer will subconsciously see the money signs behind your eyes. It will be twice as difficult – or impossible – to make the sale.

Salespeople who adopt the Win-Win principle will always earn much more than any other salesperson. They will receive an ongoing supply of referred leads from their customers and will rapidly build a reputation for being people to do business with. They never need to work out in advance how much money they will make from a sale and whether their earnings will cover their expenses. In general, they have so much money coming in that they have a problem knowing how to spend it!

Robert was a salesperson for a wholesale stationery supplies company and was constantly struggling to meet his minimum sales targets. He had set these himself to provide sufficient income to meet the mortgage repayments on his new apartment and to cover other regular outgoings.

Robert and I had a long chat during the lunch-break of a training course I had been asked to run for his company. I soon discovered that he knew precisely how much commission he made on almost every item within his very substantial catalogue. He knew precisely how many of each item he had to sell to meet his income requirements. He knew almost exactly how many of each item each of his customers ordered on a regular basis, and he knew exactly how many extra items he had to sell to make his targets. Robert was basically a walking calculating machine, going around taking orders, making sales and adding up his commission as he went. He was so intent on making money that he had very little time to think about what he could be doing for his customers and had never considered them anything but a means of making a living. No wonder he was struggling.

I knew I couldn't get Robert to alter his attitude overnight. He had been working that way for such a long time that any change would create a substantial initial drop in his income, something he could not afford. However, after half an hour we came up with a compromise and a presentation for an item in his catalogue – a display unit – that he had sold very few of previously.

We first established what improving its sales would do for him. That was simple. If he sold one of these units to every one of the customers he regularly called on, he would increase his income by 9 per cent. That excited him greatly. We then spent some time discussing what the unit would do for Robert's customers. Bearing in mind that they had seen the money signs behind his eyes for such a long time, it was obvious that they knew he was calling on them just to make money. The obvious route, therefore, was to establish a presentation that focused entirely on how much money he could make for them – and that wouldn't be too different from his current style. We collected various items of data from other salespeople in the company who had already been selling these units and restocking them on a regular basis, and then worked out a very simple presentation that suited Robert and was certainly going to suit his customers. It went like this.

Robert was to call on his customers as usual and, as well as his catalogue and order book, would carry a piece of cardboard which measured 40 × 33 cm (16 × 13 in). This was the size of the base of the display unit he was going to sell. His presentation would consist of moving a few items on the customer's sales counter until he could put the cardboard down flat in the small space he had created. He would then say, 'Mr Customer, if I could show you a way of earning £425 a year from this space, would you be interested?' Who could say no? Robert would then present the data to support his figures, promise to make sure the unit was regularly restocked and write up the order.

Robert did all this and over a three-month period his sales increased by over 18 per cent.

He and I have spent a lot more time together since. We have adapted almost every presentation he had been using before and he no longer thinks about how much a sale will make for him. His only concern is to see what else he can do for his customers so that they can make more money.

He now knows that, by doing so, he is already earning much more than he ever did before – and that as long as he continues to put his customers' interests first his income will continue to increase.

PEOPLE ONLY BUY BECAUSE THEY WANT TO

There are various reasons why people join the profession of selling. Some like the challenge and the competitive environment of most sales organizations. Other people appreciate the freedom to work how and when they wish and yet others are in the profession because they enjoy meeting people. All of them enjoy the potential there is to make a lot of money.

There is usually only one reason why someone wants to buy something from a salesperson. It is precisely that. They want to. Your job as a salesperson is therefore to make people want to buy whatever it is that you have to sell.

There can be many different reasons why people might want to buy your product or service. It is critically important that you know as many of them as possible before you can sell as many as possible. Psychoanalysis of the product or service you are selling is therefore another key element in helping you to increase your sales and thus to double your income.

The following are sixteen reasons why people might want to buy or own something. At least 75 per cent of them can be used to justify a purchase.

It is fashionable	It looks good
It is expected to own one	It is a status symbol
It improves health	It makes them feel proud
It provides security	It fulfils an ambition
It improves appearance	It is enjoyable to own

It will help to make more money	It makes life easier
It feels good	It makes life more comfortable
It makes somebody love them	It is needed

These reasons also apply if the person you are selling to is buying your product or service to sell it on to someone else. Their primary motive may be profit, but that profit will enable them to buy or be sold many other things – which will always be bought for some of the above reasons.

Study the list again carefully and see if you can add any other reasons. I doubt if you could. However, you should have noticed that, of all the reasons given for wanting to buy or own something, there is only one logical reason for making a purchase. That is the last one: somebody needs it.

People Buy for Emotional Reasons –
Not for Logical Ones

Another major lesson to be learned is that there is rarely a logical reason for buying anything. Most purchases are made for one of the emotional reasons I have listed, not because they are needed.

The salesperson who relies on a customer needing something before he or she can sell it is at the very bottom of the sales success ladder and is likely to stay there. Customers who think they need a product or service can almost invariably think of another dozen reasons why they can do without it. The salesperson who can take an interest and excite the customer's emotions is the salesperson who will very quickly get to the top of the ladder.

Your next job, therefore, is to psychoanalyse what you are selling and determine which reasons for purchasing it might apply, then to define in detail the features that provide those emotional benefits.

Let us take a few examples that will help you to psychoanalyse your product or service.

Let us assume that you sell computers. Are they fashionable? Absolutely. But why? Very simply, it is old-fashioned not to use computers. In addition, people assume that computer-based organizations are more efficient and more service orientated than non-computer-based ones. In other words, ownership and use of computers demonstrates that a company cares about its customers.

Is it expected that companies use them? Of course! Will they improve health? If they give the owner more time to play tennis, golf, swim or even just relax – yes, they will. Will they provide security? If they make a company more efficient and more profitable, the extra money will certainly help to provide more security. The company's clients will also feel more secure in the knowledge that their records are backed up daily and that copies are stored in burglarproof and fireproof safes.

Computers, especially today's modern and compact styles, do look good; and they do improve the appearance of an office. They are still status symbols – how many times have you heard someone boast that their office is now fully computerized? That also means they feel proud. Ownership probably fulfils an ambition, and computers are enjoyable to use.

So why is it that every business is not taking advantage of the benefits computerization can bring? The answer is that they have not been sold to properly. Many businesses can still manage without computers and if the emotional benefits of ownership are not sold to them they can always find a reason why they don't need them.

Not long ago, a computer salesman asked me to look at the telephone presentation he was using to make appointments to demonstrate his new office system. His market was small to medium-sized, privately owned businesses and he was not having a great deal of success in getting in front of potential clients.

During his telephone conversation he bombarded his prospects with technical data and described many of the different functions of office administration the system would deal with and the state-of-the-art presentations it could produce. He then asked for an appointment. Most of the time this was refused. Why? Simply because the average owner of a small to medium-sized business is not interested in systems for administration, presentations and handling of data. What the owner is interested in is profits and he or she needs to be sold to on that basis. Appealing to the profit motive, and the emotional results of making extra profit, is therefore essential.

We came up with a very simple telephone approach which went like this:

Mr Prospect, my company has developed a system which can increase your profits by up to 22 per cent within six weeks of adopting it. It will take me only ten minutes of your time to demonstrate this to you and you can then decide if it's appropriate for your style of management.

That salesman made a lot of appointments using this approach, sold a lot of systems which people bought for emotional reasons and, logically, he made a lot of money as a result.

It does not matter what product or service you think of, at least 75 per cent of the emotional reasons listed on pages 29 and 30 can be applied to justifying its purchase. All you, as a salesperson, have to do is go through that list and identify, and give examples of, how it will satisfy those fundamental emotional needs. If you can do that, your prospect will want to need it.

As a final example, take the following products or services and ask yourself which emotional reasons can be used to justify a purchase. Also ask yourself: if those emotional reasons did not exist, would anybody really need to buy anything?

Security systems	A new dress
A new car	A holiday
Life insurance or a pension plan	A country cottage
A new lawn-mower	Membership of the country club
A personal organizer	Garden furniture

Now take your own product or service and carefully examine the emotional reasons that might be considered by a prospective purchaser when he or she is making their decision.

Write the reasons down one at a time and expand upon each one until you can conjure up a series of verbal pictures that can be used to reinforce a buying decision. Remember that a potential buyer does this subconsciously and without realizing it. If you can define these reasons and find the one or two emotional points that really arouse each prospective purchaser you are more than half-way to doubling your income in the next few weeks.

So far this week we have discussed the principle of Win-Win and we have psychoanalysed the relationship between the buyer and the seller. We have psychoanalysed the emotional reasons why people buy and we have psychoanalysed the product or service that you are selling. Now we are going to psychoanalyse the most important part of your plan to double your income: you!

PSYCHOANALYSING YOURSELF

Because you have been carrying out your first-week exercises you already know that you are the best salesperson there is. But there is always room for improvement.

Psychoanalysis used to be considered an extremely complicated process. I am going to show you a simple definition which, in conjunction with our process of Psycho-Dynamic Programming, will solve most of the problems in your sales career.

The ultimate aim of psychoanalysis is to achieve a comprehensive insight into the various emotional or psychological processes that are causing problems in any particular area of activity. This involves a therapist helping the person under analysis to be brutally frank and honest in disclosing the problems he or she might have. Because these are frequently rooted in childhood and may involve parents and other relationships, the process is often long and difficult and admitting the problems will not always result in a cure. Often, psychoanalysis will just raise a whole new set which require further analysis. In fact, some people spend the rest of their lives on the psychiatrist's couch.

For the purpose of doubling your income, we need only consider your sales career – specifically, those aspects with which you may be, or have been, experiencing problems. We do not need to involve family, friends or other relationships, and we can certainly ignore the various childhood incidents that may have contributed to the personality you are today.

Because we are ignoring relationships, and because the only person you need to expose your various weaknesses to is yourself, you should not find it difficult to be completely honest, particularly when you accept that, whatever the problems are that may be holding you back, they can almost certainly be cured overnight using Psycho-Dynamic Programming. Have no doubt about that.

What Makes a Great Salesperson?

What are the various attributes that make a great salesperson? I shall concentrate only on the psychological points and list what I consider the most vital ones, but not necessarily in order of importance.

1 Positive thinking There is no other profession in which rejection is so likely and where the ability to think positively is therefore so vital.

2 Determination The only difference between the salesperson on the bottom rung of the ladder and the millionaire is often just having that essential extra dose of determination to succeed.

3 A good imagination Prospects are most easily converted to buyers when you can excite their imagination. It's a lot more difficult to do that if you yourself don't have one.

4 A great sense of pride in what you do Salespeople are often maligned by the public and the media and are frequently the subject of cruel jokes. Don't ever forget that without salespeople almost every other form of employment would cease.

Practically everything that is made has to be sold. Without those sales there would be little need for lawyers, accountants, tax inspectors and collectors, lorry drivers . . . If you act with integrity, you have every reason in the world to be proud. When, as I expect you to, you double your income over the next few weeks, you will have a few more reasons for pride.

5 Self-reliance You have heard the expression 'The buck stops here' before. If you are selling the right product to the right audience, you have no one but yourself to blame if you don't succeed. In the sales profession you stand or fall by your own worth. Your colleagues and your competitors are all trying to get to the top of the same pile. The only person you can really rely on is you.

6 Self-motivation Average earners get average support from their colleagues. Top people also get average support – or less. To be better than average, you cannot rely on others to motivate you. You must know what you want and have the self-motivation to go and get it.

7 The ability to get on with all types of people and develop relationships quickly and easily This is vital. People like to do business with people they like.

8 An open mind If you really want to succeed, you must be prepared to do anything that will always keep you a little bit ahead of your strongest competition. The winner of a horse race may have won only by a nose. The difference between the prize money for first and second place is enormous.

9 Confidence You must be confident not only that you can do everything necessary to achieve all your aims and ambitions, but also that you can be, and are going to be, the very best. When setting your targets find out who in your field has the highest volume of sales and earnings, and have the confidence to know that you are better than them and will do better than them. When you are that confident, everyone will want to buy from you.

10 Fearlessness Fear can be the downfall of otherwise good salespeople. A sales career involves many different aspects of work, most often simplified as prospecting, presenting, closing and record-keeping. Some of these activities may scare you and you may hesitate to do them. This must not be allowed to happen.

Which of these are your weakest points and which are the strongest? Take a clean sheet of paper and, first of all, list all your strong ones in concise, point form. Take as long as you need and give this exercise very careful consideration. When you have listed your strong points, do the same with those you consider to be your weak ones.

It is essential that you give this a great deal of thought and that you are completely honest with yourself. Apart from the attributes I have discussed above, write down and define any other problem areas you feel may be holding you back from achieving your real potential.

The following example by a former student will give you an idea of what you should be seeking to define.

My strong points
I always think positively.
I know that I can achieve all that I set out to do.
I am determined to succeed.
I am very proud of what I do to earn my living.

I get on well with all types of people and make friends easily.
I am prepared to study and devote much of my spare time to developing a winning edge.

My weak points

Although I am always positive, I sometimes get depressed when things are not going well for me. This makes me hesitate to get on with the things I know I should be doing.

I am not very good at painting pictures for people. I tend to rely on product facts in my presentation.

I often blame external factors for failure to reach my targets and often feel let down by the lack of support from my sales manager.

I get scared of prospecting. It's an area that I'm weak in.

Now, based on your analysis of your strong and weak points, you need to formulate a statement that will override the problems in your sub-conscious mind and which you will use during your periods of Psycho-Dynamic Programming this week.

This is the statement we arrived at from the example given above:

I am always positive and achieve all that I wish without any help from others. I am brilliant at prospecting and have a vivid imagination. That is why I get on so well with people and never get depressed.

Notice that there are no negative thoughts in this statement. Former weak points have been turned into strong ones and linked directly to the original strong points in order to establish a close association between them.

Now take some time to write your own statement. Take as long as you need and rewrite it as many times as you have to until it sounds good and feels good. Only when you have achieved this should you continue.

PSYCHO-DYNAMIC EXERCISES

During this week you will, of course, do your morning relaxation and visualization exercises. In addition, at the end of every evening relaxation exercise, use your statement in place of the one you used last week. Remember to repeat it over and over again for at least ten minutes after your initial relaxation and breathing exercises. Your subconscious mind will accept these statements and, by the end of the week, you will have no weak points to get in the way of doubling your income.

I also want you to adapt your visualization exercises from now onwards. During this last week you have probably thought of many different things you would like to do, places you would like to go to and objects you would like to own. Now I want you to be much more specific and detailed. Select the objectives that are most important to you and, from now on, imagine them in a great deal more detail. It is essential to realize that the more detail you put into your subconscious mind, the more your subconscious mind will be able to assist you in achieving your ambitions.

For example, if you want to own a new sports car, you need to know the make, the colour of the paintwork and upholstery, the look of the dashboard, the colour and finish on the steering-wheel and the make of tyre. In other words, everything that would enable a stranger to produce a detailed picture of what is in your mind must be listed.

If it is a new house, the same applies. You need to visualize the colour of the brickwork, the window-frames and the roof. You need to visualize the number of rooms and the decor in every one, right down to the last detail. Most important, you need to visualize yourself living there, just as you need to imagine yourself owning and driving the sports car in the previous example.

At the beginning of Week Two, you are already armed with enough tools to enable you to realize more positive results than you ever dreamed were possible. Have a really good week and, above all else, enjoy your new-found enthusiasm.

Summary of Key Points

● The principle of 'Win-Win' is a key factor in sales success.

● Unless both the buyer and the seller can benefit from a transaction, there is unlikely to be a sale.

● People only buy for one reason. Because they want to. Your job as a salesperson is to make people want to buy what you want to sell.

● People only buy for emotional reasons. They never buy for logical reasons.

● Examine your products or services and identify all the emotional reasons why someone would want to buy them.

● Identify all your weak points and strong points and formulate a statement to use with your relaxation exercises.

● When carrying out your visualization exercises, go into as much detail as you possibly can. A stranger should be able to paint an accurate picture from the detail you imagine.

● Complete your sales records for the current week.

WEEK THREE

BUYERS AND THEIR PSYCHOLOGICAL PROFILES

PSYCHO-SELLING TECHNIQUES THAT MAKE THEM WANT TO BUY

Two weeks are now over and your sales figures should be at least 12 per cent up on what they were before you started to study this book. If you're not leaping around feeling marvellously excited and eager to get started on Week Three, you should be.

If your sales had decreased by 12 per cent, you would be very depressed. If your mortgage rate had gone up by 12 per cent in the last two weeks, you would be going crazy along with the rest of the nation. As a star salesperson, you should be as excited about good news as most other people are about bad news.

PSYCHOLOGICAL PROFILES OF BUYERS

The really good news is that this week you are going to learn how to identify the various types of buyer in the market-place. You are going to learn how to psychoanalyse them and their various buying patterns, and how you need to treat each type in a selling situation. As a result, you are going to double your chances of selling to them. And guess what else? You've got it! You are going to double your chances of doubling your income!

There are several different types of potential buyer, but each of them falls into one of two very distinct categories. These are the two that we shall deal with first.

The Conceptual Buyer and the Analytical Buyer

Picture the scene. You have an appointment with the managing director of a privately owned manufacturing company whose premises are situated on a modern, purpose-built factory estate just outside town. The first thing you notice is the neat, clearly marked parking spaces in the forecourt. You pull up in the space marked 'visitors' and your eye is caught by the car parked in the space marked J. Higgins. Mr Higgins is your prospect and drives a one-year-old luxury saloon car that is very clean and obviously well maintained.

The reception area is well laid out and tidy. There are several, nicely framed reproductions of modern art on the wall. The receptionist is polite, makes you feel welcome, offers you a cup of coffee and announces your arrival to your prospect's secretary.

Ten minutes later, and that is ten minutes after your appointed time, Mr Higgins' secretary comes down to collect you and takes you up for your first meeting with Joe Higgins.

As you enter his office you quickly take in the smart, but not overly expensive, carpets and office furnishings. There are more pictures on the walls, one or two of which appear to be limited editions that have been signed by the artist. There are several golfing trophies on the bookcase and a photograph that appears to be Mr Higgins standing by a yacht and collecting a trophy.

Mr Higgins stands up to greet you with a friendly but cautious smile, extends his hand, offers a firm handshake and bids you sit down in a comfortable, upright, visitor's chair on the opposite side of the desk to himself. He is dressed smartly. He wears a fairly expensive suit, a well-ironed, pale blue shirt, a modern tie and is well groomed.

The desk itself is very neat and tidy, particularly for the owner of a medium-sized manufacturing company. There is a small pile of drawings on one side, held down by a very ornate, modern glass paperweight. Several other sketches are in front of him. A note-pad on the desk is covered with various, abstract doodles. In a corner of the office, behind the desk, is a slightly untidy pile of files. In the opposite corner, a briefcase lies open. It is literally littered with odd scraps of paper, bills, taxi receipts and other paraphernalia.

Picture another scene, very different from this. Your appointment with Mr Jones is scheduled for ten minutes past eleven, at his request. At 11.30, Mr Jones enters the reception area, mumbles an apology for being late and, without any handshake, bids you follow him to his office, promptly turns his back to you and leads the way.

Mr Jones is wearing a shabby suit that has obviously not been pressed for some time. His shoes are somewhat worn down at the heel and his hair looks as if it was last cut at about the same time that his suit was last pressed.

On entering his office you immediately notice its unkempt and untidy appearance. Everything is dowdy and looks as if it should have been replaced at least two or three years ago. There are no frills, no pictures on the wall, no magazines on the coffee-table and only technical books on the bookshelf. The desk is littered with papers in an order that is obviously logical to Mr Jones but would make little sense to anyone else. Most of them are covered with figures and various calculations. The writing is neat and precise, and all the additions appear to have been double-checked and annotated in red ink to indicate their accuracy.

These are two extreme examples of the two main categories of prospects, customers or clients that you can come across. They will not always be quite so straightforward but, by analysing each of these examples, you will in future be able to recognize the categories nine times out of ten and tailor your presentation accordingly.

Mr Higgins is a typical 'conceptual' and emotional buyer, not in the least concerned with facts or figures. He makes almost instant decisions. If he wants something, and as long as he thinks he can afford it, he will buy it. He may not even haggle over the price. Provided you hit the right emotional hot button, he will probably have talked himself into the sale long before you even attempt to close him.

Mr Higgins is concerned with overall appearances hence the cordial welcome when you first arrive, the neat and fairly expensive furnishings in his office, his smart, somewhat trendy and well-groomed appearance and the various paintings, photographs and trophies which adorn the walls and bookcase.

The other significant clues to his conceptual category are the doodles on the note-pad, the pile of files in the corner of the office and the very untidy briefcase coupled with the fairly tidy desk and the noticeable absence of very much other paperwork.

If you think Mr Higgins is a salesperson's dream, however, you could not be further from the truth. Press the wrong hot button and you could switch his interest off so quickly that, in the space of a few seconds, you might just as well be a million miles away for all the good it will do you. Try and impress him with too many facts, figures or statistics and you'll bore him so quickly that you'll never regain his interest.

As with the second of the two main categories, there are several versions of Mr Higgins. However, once you learn to recognize them, selling to them will become very much easier.

Mr Jones is, of course, the complete opposite to Mr Higgins. Mr Jones is an 'analytical' buyer. Left to his own devices, and in the absence of any salespeople to bother him, he probably wouldn't change the office carpet or furniture for another twenty years. By the time he had worked out his budgets and decided whether or not he could afford them, prices would probably have gone up – and he would anyway have thought of a dozen different reasons why he didn't need a change.

Mr Jones does not spend money unnecessarily, at least in his business life. His personal habits, however, may be very different. His office is untidy and so is he. But take a look at the columns of figures on the documents piled on his desk. You will soon realize that Mr Jones knows exactly what is happening in every part of his organization and has his finger very much on the pulse. He does not make snap decisions or snap judgements. Try to close him on an idea without any data to back it up and you will get nowhere.

Mr Jones can be an emotional buyer but, to arouse his emotions in the first place, you will have to provide a lot of technical information and other facts and figures to support your statements. Some variations of Mr Jones can actually be a lot easier to close than Mr Higgins, provided you know how to handle them.

So there we have it. Two main categories of buyer: the conceptual and the analytical. Just being able to identify these two types quickly when first meeting them can double your chances of making that sale.

It will, however, take a little time and practice before you get it right every time. The distinction between the conceptual buyer and the analytical one is not always as obvious as in the examples above. There is often a little of Mr Jones in Mr Higgins and a lot of Mr Higgins in Mr Jones and vice versa. On most occasions you won't have a great deal of time to decide.

The key, of course, is observation. You must be acutely aware of how your prospect behaves, his style of dress, the environment of his workplace where appropriate and any other factors that can help you decide instantly whether the person you are about to sell to is a conceptual or analytical buyer.

THE PSYCHOLOGICAL SUB-CATEGORIES

To give you an even greater edge, we need to examine the various other sub-categories of buyers. These are: grumpy; friendly; timid; the procrastinator; the snob; and, finally, the dealer.

The Grumpy Buyer

Grumpy buyers are obviously not very difficult to spot. They tend to be miserable and complain a lot, often about things that are totally irrelevant to your company and your sales presentation. They will almost always see the worst in any situation instead of the best, and are inclined to think that things will go wrong rather than right. They always have problems and are cautious, cost conscious and, of course, grumpy.

As well as deciding whether a grumpy buyer is conceptual or analytical, you must also learn to respond in a way that will make him or her your friend. The secret to dealing with people in this category is to be sympathetic. You must show concern for their concerns, always agree with them – provided, of course, that your agreement is based on the truth – and never argue. Arguing only makes them worse. However, almost every time you do agree and show sympathy or concern, reinforce what your product or service can do to solve their problems.

For example, let us suppose that your grumpy buyer is complaining about the recession their industry is in at the moment. Agree. When you have finished agreeing, tell him or her that you know, from your experience in the industry, that they are in fact actually doing much better than their competition. If this is stretching the truth, you could say that the particular product or service you are selling is recession proof, sells better in a recession or helps cut costs during a recession. In other words, tailor your presentation so that you agree with their concerns, soothe their worries and then sell to them on the basis of whether they are a conceptual or analytical buyer.

The Friendly Buyer

Now to the friendly buyer – everybody's friend, in fact. People in this sub-category like to be liked. They like to tell stories and to get involved in long conversations that have nothing to do with business. They are always pleased to see most people who call on them and, because they are so friendly and easy to get along with, you may think that a sale is inevitable. Nothing could be further from the truth.

The friendly buyer is more likely to use the time allotted for your meeting to enjoy a long, friendly chat, then whisk you out of the door with a hearty pat on the back, a big smile and no order. They are so good at this that, no matter how many times you call, they will do the same thing time after time and you will be powerless to stop them.

The secret of dealing with the friendly buyer is quite simple. You must, of course, be friendly. But your friendliness must be controlled. Once you have decided whether your buyer is the analytical or conceptual type, tailor your presentation accordingly and be friendly but firm. Do not allow yourself to be side-tracked into conversations that are not related to business.

Be firm and stay on track.

One of the easiest ways to deal with the friendly buyer is to imagine you are a schoolteacher admonishing a naughty, cheeky child. You know the type: friendly, full of excuses and with a great story to explain why he or she didn't have time to do their homework. It is not difficult to imagine how a schoolteacher would deal with this child. You need to do the same with your prospect. Putting him or her into that context and acting the friendly schoolteacher may get you the sale that all your competitors have failed to get. If the friendly buyer is a customer and if, instead of swapping stories, you can double the amount of time you spend selling, you will almost certainly double the order.

The Timid Buyer

Now for the timid buyer. Timid buyers are not timid because of their physical size; they come in all shapes and sizes. They are timid because of the way they think. Their one outstanding characteristic is that they are scared – of making decisions, of change, of making mistakes, of the competition. And they are absolutely petrified of you.

Nevertheless, timid buyers, once recognized, are very easy to deal with. The secret is never to scare them. This means that, above all else, you must take your time. As with the friendly buyer, you have to stay on track. But you must also slow down your sales presentation to a rate that is even slower than your prospect would like it to be. Provided you have identified his or her major type correctly, doing so will prompt them to answer questions and get involved in the sales process. They will quickly begin to feel that they are in charge, possibly for the first time ever, and will become very easy to sell to.

Once you feel that they are ready to buy, you must not offer them a choice. Remember that, above all else, timid buyers are scared of making decisions and it is therefore up to you to make decisions for them. If you feel the blue model is the best for them, or your middle-of-the-range photocopier is most suited to their needs, only offer them that particular one. Don't ask for the sale because you won't get it. Assume that they are going to buy and just write up the order, push the order form across to them and tell them to authorize it.

The Procrastinating Buyer

The procrastinator will also be obvious to you. People in this sub-category just cannot make up their minds about anything. It is not because they are scared. It is simply part of their psychological make-up.

In their private and business lives, procrastinators always ask other people's opinions and, very often, ask other people to make the decisions for them. To sell to the procrastinator, you must simply make him or her a friend. Once they are comfortable with you, they will use you as they use everyone else, and will give you the opportunity to make the decision for them. At the slightest sign of a buying signal, tell them what they should be doing– and close the sale.

The Snobbish Buyer

The snob is a totally different character. Snobs look down their noses at most people and probably consider salespeople to be a lower life-form that is hardly deserving of their time or energy. They need very careful handling.

They have two major disadvantages for you to capitalize on. First, they think they know it all, and there is no fool like a 'know all'. Second, although they pretend to know everything, deep down they are very insecure and have an avaricious need to learn. It is fatal to get into an argument with a snob, even if he or she is wrong. Snobs enjoy conflict so much that the disagreement, whatever its subject, will ruin your chances of making a sale.

The clever way to deal with snobs is to flatter them. By complimenting them on their knowledge of your product or service, and feeding back a little more information each time, you can easily lead them into a closing situation. However, you must remember that snobs never like to be sold to. You must therefore make sure that you phrase your closing question in such a way that the snob believes he or she has decided to buy.

Remember, too, that snobs like to be thanked. Thank them for seeing you, thank them for their interest, thank them for just about anything you can thank them for. Then thank them again for the order when you leave.

The Dealer Buyer

Our final category is the dealer. Dealers just love to deal. They want the very best price you can offer, the best service and the best delivery. When you have agreed to everything, and given away most of your profit, they will want even more – and there will still be no guarantee that they are going to buy from you.

Do not confuse a dealer with a negotiator. Most people like to negotiate the best offer they can for themselves. In many cases, if they are working for a company, it is their responsibility to obtain the best they can for their employer. That is what they are paid to do. A dealer's psychology is very different and dealers are unique among the categories we have discussed. They can be the toughest negotiators, but their weak spots make them the easiest category to sell to.

First, dealers do not like to waste time unnecessarily. If they start to deal, even on very minor points during your initial approaches, they must be interested in what you have to offer. Second, they have an over-abundance of pride, and hate to go back on their word once they have given it. Third, they tend to be in a hurry. To secure a sale with a dealer, you need to arouse his or her interest, create a sense of urgency and get a commitment at every single stage of your presentation. You will then always be able to take a step back in your negotiation and remind them that they made that commitment. They will rarely go back on their word.

Once you have decided whether the dealer is a conceptual or analytical buyer, and provided you follow the simple sequence of arousing interest, creating urgency and getting frequent commitments, you will have more fun dealing with the dealer than with any other type of prospect. In addition, because of their nature, dealers tend to hold some of the most powerful positions in trade and industry and have some of the largest purchasing budgets. Learn to deal with the dealer and you can easily become one of the highest paid people in sales.

In the following chapters we will deal in detail with the three main areas involved in the sales process: prospecting, presenting and closing. However, this week, as well as showing you how to identify the various prospect types, I am going to teach you a very simple technique that will work well no matter what prospect type you are dealing with, and which will enable you to make some extra sales.

ESTABLISHING IMMEDIATE RAPPORT

Every salesperson knows, or should know, that when you first meet a prospective customer or client you have only a few short minutes to establish some form of rapport. Many people will tell you that the sale is made or lost in those minutes. If you are successful, it can be the start of a long and profitable relationship. If you get it wrong, you will probably lose that prospect – and, for some people, good prospects are often hard to find.

So what is the secret of establishing an immediate rapport with a potential buyer? I learned a long time ago that, subconsciously, everyone likes to do business with someone as similar to themselves as possible. People may admire their opposites and want to be like them but, until they are, they prefer not to do business with them. They simply feel more comfortable with somebody who is just like them.

The key to establishing an immediate rapport with a potential buyer is therefore to make them believe that you are as similar to them as possible. Once you have achieved this they will want to do business with you and will never know that they have been Psycho-Sold.

Up to now, you have been programming your own subconscious mind using the techniques of Psycho-Dynamic Programming. To establish an immediate rapport with your prospect, it is no use talking to their conscious mind – you would appear to be quite stupid if, having just met him or her, you suddenly announced that you were 'just like them'. Even if you did, they would be most unlikely to believe you. The secret is to talk to the prospect's subconscious mind. You can't do this with words but you can use a much more powerful tool: mimicry.

The Art of Mimicry

If you have ever watched a professional mime artist you will probably have been spellbound. You are unlikely to have noticed that, during the act, the voice in your head that normally holds an ongoing conversation with your conscious mind tends to stop. Instead, you feel the performance. It's a similar situation when you close your eyes while listening to music. With your eyes open, there are many visual distractions. When you close them, the music seems to be much clearer, almost as if you are hearing it with another part of your brain. In both of these examples, it is the subconscious mind that has taken over a significant part of the identification, analysis and enjoyment of the performance.

The art of using mimicry in Psycho-Selling allows you to get in direct contact with your prospect's subconscious mind, and is one of the most powerful and dynamic tools you will ever learn. It is an extremely simple technique. All you need to do from the moment that you meet your prospect is mimic as many of his or her actions as you possibly can, as quickly as you can.

If you are greeted with a firm handshake, respond with a firm one. If the handshake is weak, yours must also be weak. If your prospect remains standing with a hand in their pocket, you remain standing with a hand in your pocket. If your prospect sits forward in their chair, you sit forward. If they sit with their arms folded, never mind what you have been told about body language in the past – you sit with your arms folded. Reverse mimicry, which I'll deal with later, will get them to uncross them.

If you are offered tea or coffee, choose what your prospect chooses. It doesn't matter if you hate three spoons of sugar in your tea, it's worth putting up with if it will help you close that sale. The fact that you are drinking the same beverage as your prospect, no matter how revolting you may find it, will do much to tell their subconscious mind that you are similar to them – and that they like you.

If your prospect crosses their legs, you cross yours. If he or she starts to fiddle with a pen, do the same. Everything you do during the course of your meeting with a prospective client that mimics what he or she is doing will help to cement a relationship with that person more quickly than anything else.

In case you're thinking what I think you're thinking – no! You will never be spotted. I have mastered this technique and can almost mirror what the other person is doing. I have never been found out. The more like someone you are, the less likely they are to notice it. However, their subconscious mind will be noticing all the time. And it will be telling them that they like you, that they trust you and that they would like to do business with you. From there on the sale should be just a formality.

How many times have you come back from a meeting and your only excuse for not closing the sale has been that you just could not get on with the prospect? There was probably something different about you that his or her subconscious could not deal with. By using the art of mimicry, you will almost always establish an immediate rapport with a prospect, and you will almost always do business with them.

I explained this technique to a book publisher one morning. She was very concerned about a lunch meeting she was having with a buyer from a major department store. In the past, he had always been very difficult to get on with and reluctant to place more than just a small order with her.

The publisher called me back later that day. She told me that she had tried, but found it very difficult, to copy the buyer's mannerisms. She had, however, not found it difficult to order the same food and drink as her prospect. Apparently, by the time the dessert trolley came around and she ordered the strawberries and cream, without sugar, as her prospect had, he was virtually eating out of her hand. She came away with the biggest order she had ever received from that buyer and, in addition, developed a completely different relationship with him that, over the next few years, made her a great deal of money.

I often tell my clients that nobody has ever made any money by saying 'no'. You only have a chance to make it when you agree to do something. Doing nothing can only get you nowhere. Therefore, as well as using your new-found skills in prospect analysis, try using the art of mimicry on every person you see this week. I guarantee you will find the results amazing not only in business but also in your personal life. I have known people treble their income in one week by using just this one aspect of Psycho-Selling.

Reverse Mimicry

Now let's take the art of mimicry one step further. Learn to master reverse mimicry and you will be able to exercise a degree of control over potential customers that you never dreamed was possible.

I discovered this additional technique quite by accident one day. I was with a customer who obviously needed the product I was selling. On occasions like these, when the sale looks as if it is going to be fairly easy to secure, I often use the time to practise, and experiment with, some of my sales techniques. I was mimicking everything my customer was doing and we were getting along very well together. All of a sudden, I had an irresistible urge to scratch the side of my nose, and did so. To my surprise, so did my customer.

I assumed that this was just a coincidence but, just in case, I placed my hand on the top of his desk and played with the corner of my catalogue which was lying there. Within seconds, my customer was playing with the corner of his copy of my catalogue. In no time at all, I was able to switch from mimicking what he was doing to getting him to do almost anything I wanted him to do.

Imagine just how powerful this technique can be. Suppose you are selling a product that has a wonderful feel to it. If you were to ask your prospect's conscious mind to touch and feel it, he or she would naturally be suspicious that you were trying to sell them something – after all, you are. When you use the art of reverse mimicry, you get their subconscious mind to act and enjoy the feel of your product. As you have already learned, the subconscious is a lot more powerful than the conscious mind.

The techniques of mimicry and reverse mimicry are a little like fishing. You first mimic your client to reel them in a little then, when they are fairly well hooked, you use reverse mimicry to get their subconscious to accept your product or service and do some more selling for you. If your client starts to get away, you revert to mimicry again, and so on.

For the rest of this week, practise identifying prospect types, the art of mimicry and, if you feel confident, reverse mimicry.

PSYCHO-DYNAMIC EXERCISES

Do your morning and evening exercises. I also want you to do the following exercise every evening after your initial relaxation period.

Imagine the perfect sale that will provide you with the maximum amount of money or reward. Imagine in detail every stage of the sales process from the moment you walk in to the moment you leave with the order. Do not miss out any single detail. Repeat this exercise over and over again every evening. By doing so, you will be programming your subconscious to expect the sale to happen – and your subconscious will make it happen, with no further help from you.

Have a great week!

Summary of Key Points

● There are two main categories of buyer. These are the conceptual and the analytical buyer. The key to identifying these two categories is observation.

● There are six sub-categories of buyers. They are classified as grumpy, friendly, timid, procrastinators, snobs and dealers. These categories are usually easily identifiable.

● The secret of establishing an immediate rapport with a client is to use the art of mimicry. This is one of the most powerful techniques of psycho-selling.

● Once learned, the technique of reverse mimicry can help you make a client do whatever you want him or her to do.

● This week's exercise after your evening relaxation period is to imagine the perfect sales presentation in as much detail as possible, thus programming your subconscious to create opportunities.

● Enter your sales records for the current week.

WEEK FOUR

PERFECT PROSPECTS
HOW TO IDENTIFY THEM AND MAKE THEM COME TO YOU

PSYCHO-PROSPECTING

Every salesperson needs somebody to sell to. These potential buyers are called prospects. Unless you work in an area of sales where prospective clients literally walk in off the street and demand details of your product or service, you will have to go and look for them. No prospects – no sales!

Some salespeople I have met have had the potential to be the greatest in the profession but have never earned a living simply because they never learned how to prospect effectively for new clients. In the last part of this chapter I will show you how to make the perfect prospect, your ideal customer or client, appear almost miraculously in front of you. However, you will not be able to achieve this until you have examined the psychology of prospecting.

WHO DO YOU WANT TO SELL TO?

I have already discussed the fact that people like to do business with people they like. Why should it not be the same for you? If you are going to sell for a living, you might as well enjoy it. Therefore, why not start off by making a simple rule? If you have to prospect, look for people you would like to do business with. Let's examine this a little more carefully.

Why would you like to do business with a particular person? I can think of a number of good reasons. The first, and most obvious, is that if you are successful in selling to him or her you are presumably going to earn money. Money enables you to buy the things you would like to buy and live your life in the style you wish to live it in.

Another reason could be that the prospective client moves in the same social or business circle as you do, or would like to do. If you already move in it yourself, you are naturally going to feel more comfortable with that person – and if it is a section of the business community, there will be existing customers or clients who can confirm the quality of your product or service. If it is a social circle, friends and acquaintances can endorse your honesty and integrity. All this makes it easier for you to do business with that prospect.

On the other hand, if the prospect moves in a section of the business or social community with which you are not familiar, there are other advantages in wanting to do business with him or her. The most obvious is that they will be a potential source of introductions if you do a good job for them.

Another, and very important, reason for wanting to do business with a particular person is that you know it is going to be easy. Personally, I cannot think of any better reason. The easier it is to do business with somebody, the better I like it.

It could be very difficult to sell a car to someone who had just lost their driving licence. It could be even more difficult to sell any type of electrical appliance to someone who was not connected to an electricity supply. It would be very silly to try and sell a radio to a deaf person or a book to a blind one and you would have to be completely mad to try and sell a pair of running-shoes to someone with no legs. These are extreme examples, you might say, and of course you would not attempt to do any of these things. Nevertheless, many salespeople waste much of their time trying to sell something to somebody who cannot use it, cannot afford it or who simply does not have the authority to buy it.

Qualification Is the Key

The key to successful prospecting is therefore to qualify exactly who you want to do business with and ensure that they can use your product or service, can afford it and have the authority to buy it. That is standard textbook prospecting. The golden key is the factor I mentioned at the beginning of this chapter: the ideal prospect is someone who, in addition to fulfilling all these criteria, is exactly the type of person you would like to do business with.

The more exactly you can define your potential clients or customers, the easier it will be to find them.

At first glance, you may feel that by defining your prospect so strictly you are restricting the number of potential buyers. That is not an unreasonable assumption. However, years of experience have taught me that the complete opposite is true. The more specifically you can define your target audience, the more likely you are to find it. In addition, instead of limiting your market you are, in fact, enlarging it. Why? Simply because if you can identify the perfect customer or client he or she is likely to give you many times more business than a dozen or more imperfect ones. Put another way, if you go fishing for salmon you get a bucketful in one go. If you go fishing for sprats you will need several dozen to fill a bucket. Defining the people who are likely to be your best prospects will ultimately save a lot of wasted time and effort which will allow you to concentrate on what you do best – selling.

I cannot define your perfect client for you. I do not know what your financial aims are, other than that you want to double your income. I do not know your friends or business acquaintances, or their friends and acquaintances. I do not know the product or service you are trying to sell, who could place the biggest orders or who would be in the best position, having been sold, to recommend you to other customers. However, I do know that, given some very careful consideration, it should not take you long to identify your ideal client profile for yourself.

If you have an hour or so, do it now. If not, stop reading and do not continue until you have the time to think about this.

Define Your Business

First, ask yourself what business you are in. Think about this carefully. The business you perceive yourself to be in may not be the one your ideal potential prospect sees, or wants, you to be in. You should be able to describe your activities in different ways to suit various types of prospect. For example, if you sell shoes are you a shoe salesman, a footwear consultant or in the fashion business? If you sell swimming-pools are you a swimming-pool contractor, in the water sports design business or in the leisure industry? If you sell life assurance and investment programmes are you a life insurance salesperson, an investment adviser or a financial planner? Work out as many different ways as you can to describe what you sell.

Define Your Perfect Prospect

Next, define your perfect client or customer. If your product or service is sold to businesses, what type of business is most likely to need what you are offering and can afford to buy it? Is it large corporations, privately owned companies, small businesses or professional practices? Where are they likely to be based? What businesses are most likely to buy and which would you most like to sell to? Who in those organizations is the person to make your presentation to, and does he or she have the authority to make a buying decision?

If your product or service is aimed at private individuals as opposed to businesses, who is your perfect prospect? Does he or she work? If so, what do they do and where do they do it? How much do they earn? Where do they live? How many children do they have? What schools do the children go to? What cars do they drive, where do they take their holidays, where do they shop, where do they eat, what do they do in their spare time?

Have you got the picture? That is precisely what you need to have: a complete picture of your perfect prospect in your mind. It should be so clear that if you were woken up at two o'clock in the morning you could immediately describe him or her without thinking.

Now that you have defined your perfect prospect, you have to find him or her.

To my mind, there are only two types of prospect: warm and cold. I shall deal with the latter first. Cold prospecting equates to hard work. A cold prospect is someone you currently do not know and who does not know you. You therefore have no idea whether they qualify as your ideal client or customer, and have to do a great deal of research before even attempting to arrange a meeting. Cold prospecting is a laborious, expensive and often disappointing way of looking for new business. If you intend to double your income, it is not for you.

WARM PROSPECTS

Warm prospects are a very different proposition. They are people whom you either know or who know of you, or who can be introduced to you by someone they know. They can be effectively targeted in a variety of ways. The most important thing to remember about warm prospects is that they can be qualified much more easily than cold ones as your ideal prospect. You are five times as likely to secure an appointment with a warm prospect and twice as likely to do business with them. In terms of doubling your income, it obviously makes sense to concentrate your efforts on identifying them.

Referred Leads

The very best sources of warm prospects are known as referred leads. A referred lead is simply someone you did not know who has been introduced to you by someone you do know.

The best sources of referred leads are obviously your existing clients or customers. Ideally, they should be satisfied with what you have done for them or sold to them, they should be enthusiastic about your product or service and, with a little prompting from you, should be prepared to introduce you to a number of other people who respect their opinions and are therefore likely to agree to meet you.

Obtaining referred leads is an art in itself. You will have to sell your client or customer on the idea of introducing you to prospects almost as cleverly as you sold them their original purchase. Therefore, if you are going to take the time and trouble to develop the art of obtaining referred leads, make sure they are of the right quality.

You spent some time identifying and describing your ideal prospect. I asked you to do that for a very important reason. The average salesperson who asks for referred leads puts little thought or effort into his or her presentation. A typical request will often be along the following lines: 'Can you please give me the names of three or four other people who you think may be interested in what I've sold you?'

What is wrong with that statement? After all, you have asked for exactly what you want. Or have you? Psycho-Salespeople know better. Consider that the average person knows an awful lot of people. Some are family, others are close friends. Many will be from their workplace or other people's workplaces. Your client or customer may belong to clubs or other organizations. If you were to ask him or her to list everybody they knew they would not do it, could not do it and, frankly, if they did, all you would end up with is a long list of unqualified people. Asking someone to give you the names of people they know who might be interested in your product or service just won't work. In most cases, your source of referred leads will dry up completely and be unable to think of anybody, simply because there is nothing for them to focus on.

You have defined your perfect prospect in your own mind, and that is exactly what you should ask for – you already know that this ideal client should have an interest in what you have to offer. In addition, and equally important, you enable your source to focus on a particular type of person and their subconscious mind can sort through its databank and come up with exactly the prospect you are looking for.

What else was wrong with the request? Quite simply – nobody likes to be 'sold' anything. Your choice of words is critical in your sales presentation, and just as important when asking for referred leads. People are happy to 'invest' in your service or product, they will be happy to 'acquire' it or 'own' it, they should be delighted they 'decided to buy it'. However, they will not be happy if they thought they had been sold it, and are most unlikely to introduce you to anybody if they thought you were going to try and sell something to them. We shall spend more time discussing the choice of words, and their power, later in this chapter.

How should that first request for referred leads have been presented? This is my suggestion: 'Mr Customer, you made a very wise choice when you decided to invest in our improved widget-washer. The energy savings alone could reduce the overhead costs on your factory premises by 10 per cent this year, as well as increasing your productivity and profit. You are obviously happy with the acquisition. Tell me, which of your current suppliers owns their own company, is trying to improve their profitability, is within our service area and is forward-thinking enough to be interested in a demonstration?'

What did we achieve with this request? We flattered the client by telling him he was wise, prudent and forward-thinking. We resold the benefits of our product. And we clearly defined the profile of the person we want to meet. We also removed another major psychological barrier to obtaining referred leads. We asked for the names of people the client purchased from rather than ones he sold to. This is a very important psychological factor. Your customer or client is likely to be far more willing to introduce you to somebody they buy from than to somebody they sell to. After all, they would not want you going around upsetting their customers, would they? In addition, your new prospect is much more likely to see you if a customer or client had insisted that they do so. Let's face it, who wants to upset customers?

Let's try another example. You sell family power-boats. How many referred leads do you think the following statement would get you? 'That's a great boat you just bought. Can you introduce me to two or three other people who would be interested in buying one?' I suspect you would get no leads at all.

Now look at the following role play.

Me: *Mr Jones, thank you for your custom. That boat is going to prove to be one of the best investments you've made and I'm sure your family are going to love it. Tell me, do you have a permanent mooring or do you intend to trailer it?*

Customer: We'll trailer it during our summer holidays but most of the year we will have it moored at our local yacht club. In fact, I'm taking it down next weekend.

Me: *There are going to be some very envious faces. How many members do you have?*

Customer: We have sixty-five families there and there are certainly going to be some jealous people. Joe Green will eat his heart out.

Me: *Who's Joe Green?*

Customer: He's Chairman of the Committee and he's been talking about buying one of these for about eighteen months.

Me: *It sounds as though you have a really friendly club there. I'll tell you what I would like to do. If you are launching it next Saturday, I would like to put on a little launch ceremony for you at the club. I'll bring a few bottles of champagne and perhaps you could introduce me to some of the other members. Would that be possible?*

Customer: Certainly. That won't be any problem. In fact, I'm so looking forward to launching it, let's have a proper party. You bring the drinks and I'll have my wife bring a cold buffet. Let's show the other members how to launch this beauty in style.

That episode really did happen, and would you like to know how many people I met that day? Bob Jones invited the whole club to his launch party. I had my company's banner over the drinks buffet, and by the end of that morning I had met most of the members. By the end of the summer I had sold another five boats and earned nearly enough to buy one for myself.

Those two examples illustrate just how important it is to put as much effort into your presentation to obtain referred leads as you put into making a sale. They also demonstrate how, by careful questioning, you can exactly target your ideal prospect.

Most top salespeople, and all Psycho-Salespeople, have a planned presentation for their product and know how to adapt it to the various types of buyer. They also have planned presentations for obtaining warm, referred leads.

Write your own presentation for obtaining referred leads for your product or service. Do two or three different versions. Practise them, adapt them, become fluent with them and then go and get them.

Although it is always easiest to obtain warm referred leads from a person straight after they have been sold to, when they are at their most enthusiastic, there are still countless other opportunities for obtaining them. How about people you have sold to in the past? Go back and see them. Ask if they are still as delighted with, and enthusiastic about, your product or service as they were when they first bought it. If they are not, sell it to them again. Get them enthusiastic again. When they are (or if they always have been), go through your presentation for referred leads – and don't come away without a list of at least three potential new buyers.

PEOPLE YOU FAILED TO SELL

How about people you failed to sell to previously? Even if they did not buy from you themselves, they may well know other, potentially interested persons. And with the new skills you have already learned from this book, you may well find that the people who turned you down before will buy from you this time around. You have the potential this week to make a huge increase in your sales volumes.

THE MARKET SURVEY

Another very simple way to obtain referred leads from existing clients or customers who buy from you on a regular basis is the market survey or customer satisfaction approach. We have a rule in our office that every three months every customer is called up on the telephone and asked if they are satisfied with the service they are receiving. We also ask if there is anything we can do to improve it and if there is anything else they would like us to be doing for them.

We do this for several reasons. First of all, we do genuinely care about our customers and want to maintain the standards of service that we provide. We are also keen to find out what else they would like us to do. That can make more money for us. Once we have demonstrated our care and concern, it is very easy to ask who else they know in a similar business to their own, with their level of buying power, who might be interested in doing business with us. This technique takes only a few minutes on the telephone and we generally pick up several new customers a month. How good is your after-sales service? Maybe you don't think you need to provide one in your particular field? Maybe you are wrong? Let me give you another example.

Most products that are sold today are almost obsolete even before they first become available. The research involved in development and the planning for manufacturing, advertising and all the other activities involved in a product's launch take months and months of hard work. Even as this new, improved model comes on the market the next new, improved model is almost half-way down the production line.

Two years ago I bought a new hi-fi system from a local high street store. They happily took my money. They did not take my name and address. Last week, while passing a different high street store, I noticed a far superior version of my previous purchase, at less than the cost of the original one. I went in, had a demonstration, was impressed and bought it. Think about this. If the store that I made my original purchase from had set up a simple system whereby they recorded the names, addresses and telephone numbers of their customers and the item they purchased, they would have had a wonderful opportunity to mail me or call me with details of that new, improved model at less than the cost of the old one. How many more sales would they have generated? How many stores do that? Not a lot!

What business are you in, and could you generate more sales by keeping in touch with customers when this is not considered normal practice? Once you start to provide this type of service you will not have to ask for referred leads. You will create such an impression that your customers will refer new ones to you without you asking.

Referred leads are your guarantee of sales success. By using the above methods to obtain them you can more than double your income over the next few weeks.

THE 'NEW TOWN' APPROACH

Now let us look at another way of achieving some very fast results this week. Imagine you have just moved to a completely strange town in a part of the country you have never been to before. You are going to have to find places to buy food, clothes and all sorts of household items. You will need somewhere to get your car serviced and buy petrol, a nursery to buy plants for your garden, restaurants to take your family or business contacts to. The list is endless. Spend some time now making a list of all the items or services you currently purchase.

If I had arrived in that new town I would have done precisely that. I would then have driven around and found out who the local suppliers were and which of them were most likely to be potential clients. I would visit these prospects and explain that I was new to the town. I would tell them what I did, and that it was likely I would spend a lot of money with them over the coming years. I would also explain that I prefer, whenever possible, to give my business to people who are likely to do business with me. I would be very friendly, very polite but very firm. I would get a lot of business, and give a lot.

You probably have not just moved, but you are currently giving your hard-earned money to a lot of people who could do business with you. I suspect the reason they are not doing so is because you haven't asked them. This week, go and see those people you buy from and who could buy from you. Be friendly, polite and firm. Ask for the opportunity to tell them what you do and how your product or service could benefit them. If they value your custom they will give you a hearing. The rest is up to you and the Psycho-Selling skills you have learned so far.

There are several other ways of obtaining leads and prospecting for them should be an essential and ongoing part of any sales professional's routine.

ASSOCIATING MAKES SENSE

Let's look at the word 'professional'. Selling is a profession, yet many salespeople regard it as just a job. That is the wrong psychology. Professional salespeople are as much professionals as lawyers, accountants and doctors. Lawyers, accountants and doctors have to study constantly to keep up to date with new laws, new taxes and new research. Like them, you too need to study. That is why you are reading this book. Most professionals belong to an association in order to keep in touch with developments in their field. Most salespeople don't have an association to belong to. However, they have something better: lots of other organizations and associations that they can join and become involved with – and where they can meet many new potential customers and clients.

What associations and organizations do your ideal potential buyers belong to? Make enquiries and identify one or two. Join them, get involved with them and get to know the members. Over a period of time it will become almost natural for people you meet this way to do business with you.

Joining associations and organizations is a medium-term method of prospecting. There are several others.

Obviously, you are not the only person in sales. Thousands of other salespeople are out there talking to customers and clients. Are they talking to the type of person that you would like to be talking to?

Develop a Contact Club

Developing a Contact Club over the next few months could be a very important prospecting tool for you and some other people in the selling profession. The first thing to do is identify other, non-competitive, companies that employ salespeople and that target customers very similar to your ideal prospect. When you have identified a company, telephone the sales director. Explain that you are planning to form a Contact Club and ask for the name of one of their very best salespeople. Contact that person.

The idea is to put together a small team of top salespeople from companies that are not in competition with each other but which have similar target markets. You meet once a week or once a fortnight, for breakfast or lunch, and each person is committed to bringing in the names, telephone numbers and profiles of at least two people they have sold to in the intervening period who might be appropriate contacts for you and one or two others in the group. If these potential clients are carefully chosen and matched to suitable club members they are likely to respond well to an introduction from their original contact. This should enable you to meet at least another two or three new prospects after each Contact Club meeting.

YOUR CENTRE OF INFLUENCE

Who is the most influential person you know? If you think they are influential and important, so do others. If the person is in business, he or she is likely to want to do more business. This is the start of your new network. More selling is done by networking than by almost any other means. And here I do not mean networking as applied to multi-level selling of a product. I mean networking you!

Explain to your centre of influence that you are developing a new network of business people who want to be involved in selling their products or services to others in the network, and who are prepared to help these others to sell their products or services to yet other people. Every successful person wants to do more business – and wants to do it with other successful people. They also know that business is done more easily, more efficiently, more enjoyably and more profitably if it is mutually understood that reciprocation is expected.

Everyone has their own small group of people who they try to help and who will try to help them. By formalizing this approach you can rapidly expand your network. This will in turn lead you into other networks, enabling you to reach many more people with whom you can do business, and whom you can help to do business.

'PLEASE' AND 'THANK YOU'

Earlier in this chapter I mentioned the importance of words. There are three that are frequently forgotten – and that are very important if you are going to be successful: 'please' and 'thank you'.

If this surprises you, it should not. Let's take the word 'please' first. How many times do people really use it in today's hectic and competitive business world? When was the last time someone said it to you, other than when they wanted you to do something really out of the ordinary? 'Please' is heard so infrequently in the course of day-to-day business transactions that when it is used it has a lot of impact.

'Please' conveys so many emotive messages to the recipient's subconscious mind. Warmth, harmony, co-operation, friendship, help, politeness, caring and willingness are just a few that are automatically associated with the word. When you say 'please' you are five times more likely to get the co-operation for which you are looking.

Compare the following simple requests:

Salesman One: Can I help you?
Salesman Two: *Can I help you please?*

It's obvious, is it not? The use of that one single word, accompanied by a smile, totally changes the structure, sound and feel of the request. It demonstrates a genuine concern to help, and is received warmly as opposed to creating a very positive fear of being sold to.

Now compare the next two statements, using some of the techniques you have already learned, together with the word 'please'.

Salesman One: Can you introduce me to two or three people in your neighbourhood who might be interested in buying this type of equipment?
Salesman Two: *Mr Client, I like to spend as much of my time as I can looking after my existing customers and as little time as possible looking for new ones. I would be very grateful if you could introduce me to four or five people in your neighbourhood who might also be interested in a demonstration of this equipment. Could you do that please?*

In future, add 'please' to the end of almost every request you make. You cannot overdo it, and you have nothing to lose and everything to gain.

'Thank you', delivered with a gracious smile and a warm handshake after making a sale, will make sure you are rarely forgotten. 'Thank you' after obtaining referred leads and another 'thank you' after you have done business with those leads will guarantee a steady flow of new business. A handwritten note with a simple 'Thank you for the introduction', will raise your credibility and status beyond measure.

POWER WORDS

There are some other very powerful words and this week, and for the next few weeks, I shall want you to change the format of your morning and evening exercises. Before I explain these changes, study the following list of words carefully.

ACHIEVEMENT	CONCENTRATION	HEALTH
COMMITMENT	POWER	PEACE
HARMONY	GOODWILL	FREEDOM
JUSTICE	GUIDANCE	WISDOM
INSPIRATION	INTELLIGENCE	PERSISTENCE
VITALITY	ACTIVITY	SUCCESS
PURPOSE	MASTERY	FAITH
UNDERSTANDING	CONFIDENCE	STRENGTH

Now take one word at a time and think about it for a few moments. Rely on your intuition and decide whether you feel comfortable and in tune with it or whether, subconsciously, it makes you feel slightly uncomfortable.

When you have done this with all the words, take a sheet of paper and make your own list. Divide the words into groups of two and write them side by side. The first should be a word you feel comfortable and in tune with, the second a word you feel uncomfortable about.

PSYCHO-DYNAMIC EXERCISES

Each morning spend only ten minutes on your relaxation exercise. By now, because you have been doing your exercises regularly, you are able to tap into your subconscious mind that much faster. After this ten minutes I want you to think carefully about the first word in one of your groups of two. This is the one you are comfortable with. Think about how it is part of you and part of your life. Think how inspiring it is, what it means to you in relation to your work and your relationships. Imprint the word with all its power indelibly in your subconscious. After ten minutes, take the second word. It is also powerful.

Think of the connections between it and the first word. Think about how this second word, and your acceptance of it, will enrich your life and help you to achieve your aims and ambitions. Do this for a full ten minutes.

It is important to remember that, as with all the other exercises, it does not matter if your mind wanders provided that when you realize this has happened you go back to what your were supposed to be doing.

Psycho-Dynamic Programming with power words will enable you to become more powerful in all that you do, in all aspects of your life – and, in particular, in your goal to double your income. Each day for the next few weeks select a different pair of power words to work with each morning. By the end of the next five weeks you will be amazed at the change in your attitude to life and at your ability to cope with almost anything.

I promised you that this week I would show you how to make your ideal prospect appear, almost as if out of thin air. Now is the time.

At the end of the day, when you carry out your evening relaxation exercise, reduce the relaxation time to fifteen minutes. After this period, think back to when you defined your perfect prospect. Then imagine him or her walking up to you and shaking hands. Recall all the details of your prospect, and then elaborate still further. Picture their office or home, the way they dress, what they do in their spare time. Imagine them in perfect detail. Imagine your presentation – a perfect presentation. Imagine your prospect nodding at everything you say, smiling, accepting your suggestions and buying whatever it is you are offering. Do this for a full fifteen minutes. I guarantee that if you do this properly every evening you will have met at least two perfect prospects by the end of this week.

Summary of Key Points

● There are no sales without prospects to sell to.

● Define in detail your perfect customer or client, and prospect for them.

● You must always prospect for warm leads.

● The best prospects are referred leads.

● Asking for referred leads requires the same skills as selling. Practise your presentation for obtaining them.

● Your exercise in the morning is to programme your subconscious with power words.

● Your exercise in the evening is to put the image of your perfect prospect in your subconscious.

● Enter your sales records for the current week.

WEEK FIVE

PSYCHO-SELLING TELEPHONE TECHNIQUES AND PRESENTATIONS

PSYCHO-DEPERSONALIZATION

Psycho-depersonalization can quadruple your chances of making a sale using cold calling techniques. I have known several salespeople who have become millionaires as a result of learning this amazing technique – one of the most exciting you will ever have come across – from me.

Almost every salesperson, no matter how experienced, bold and eager, can and does suffer from the fear of rejection. There is no time when you are more likely to be rejected than when making cold telephone calls. I have seen some of the very best salespeople freeze at the start of a cold calling session. I am sure you have also experienced this. You delay the start for as long as possible. You have another cup of coffee, another cigarette if you smoke, shuffle some papers and welcome an interruption from a colleague that, under normal circumstances, you would not tolerate. All due to the fear of rejection.

'Psycho-Depersonalization' is a bit of a mouthful to say, but the technique is very simple to learn. It will remove all fear of rejection and the emotions associated with it, get the potential customer or client on your side and enable you to use third party endorsements to make the prospect want to see you. Does this sound like a miracle? I can assure you that it works like one – all you have to do is try it and see.

You presumably have a telephone script that you use. The first thing to do is depersonalize it. In other words, you are not going to be you! You are going to pretend to be someone else who is calling on your behalf. For example, your script may start off like this: 'Good morning Mr Jones, my name is Mr King from Alpha Insurance Services, do you have a moment for me to explain why I am calling?' To depersonalize it, you rewrite it to say:

Good morning Mr Jones, my name is Roger Taylor and I'm calling on behalf of Mr King from Alpha Insurance Services. Do you have a few moments for me to explain why I have been asked to call?

What have we achieved so far? First, and you will soon prove this for yourself, you have psychologically removed yourself from the picture. If you have not managed to make an appointment by the time a call has finished, I promise you will not feel rejected. You will have no hesitation in getting straight on to the next one. There will be no decrease in your enthusiasm and you will not look for reasons not to pick up the telephone and dial again. The rejection will not be your problem. Your subconscious will pass the problem on to the fictitious Mr Taylor.

What else have we achieved? Mr Jones is more likely to listen to what you have to say than if he thought he was speaking directly to Mr King. If he was speaking directly to Mr King, it is likely he would be speaking directly to a 'salesman'. He would therefore feel threatened, uncomfortable and eager to get off the hook. Because he is speaking to Mr Taylor, who is calling on behalf of Mr King, he feels neither. Instead, he feels detached from any threat and is more likely to be interested in what else you have to say. In other words, you are over the first hurdle. This technique works just as well in getting you past the secretary and through to your prospect in the first place.

You now go on to your presentation. In the case of Mr Taylor and Mr Jones it may continue like this:

Mr Jones, Mr King has developed an improved and very effective plan for sheltering income from taxes. He has asked me to call you and book a short ten-minute presentation which will enable you to decide immediately if it might be appropriate for you.

That's a very good presentation. What is Mr Jones likely to ask next? It's obvious that his response will either be a request for further information or an attempt to close down the conversation. This is where the other advantages of Psycho-Depersonalization come in. Let us take them one at a time.

Mr Jones: Can you tell me more about it?

Mr Taylor: *I'm afraid not, Mr Jones. I act as Mr King's personal assistant but I'm not the expert. However, I can tell you that Mr King is probably one of the most experienced consultants that I have ever worked for. He has a degree in economics and accountancy, has been developing new tax-planning ideas throughout his career and, according to my records, nine out of ten people that he gives this ten-minute presentation to ask him to come back and see them again. I am sure it would be worth ten minutes of your time. Don't you agree Mr Jones?*

If Mr Jones had tried to decline to make an appointment, Mr Taylor would just have needed to substitute 'I am sure that it would be worth ten minutes of your time', for 'I'm afraid not, Mr Jones' and then go on to the prepared script, starting with 'I can tell you . . .' He would almost certainly get an appointment.

What have we achieved? First, that as Mr Taylor you cannot give the technical advice. Your prospect will have to see Mr King if he wants to know more – and he is obviously interested or he would not have requested further information. Second, you have a third party endorsement. As Mr King you could not possibly blow your own trumpet in the way that Mr Taylor, your employee, can blow it for you. Mr Taylor will get at least four times as many appointments for Mr King as Mr King could ever get for himself.

If you ever intend to make a cold telephone call again or if, having read this far, you can't wait to try, put the book down right now and rewrite your own script. Cold calling can be successful and fun – and it can help you double your income.

PERFECT PRESENTATIONS

It is very rare for someone to walk in and want to buy your product or service. If you are lucky and they do, you should not take that order. If they are interested enough to want to buy, you as a Psycho-Salesperson should be more than capable of selling them the new and improved version, or a better alternative to what they thought they wanted. The customer will be better off with the improved model and that new and more expensive version is presumably going to earn you more money. To sell the alternative, you will have to make a presentation.

The genuine walk-in-off-the-street prospect is a rare bird indeed. Most salespeople with the potential for very high earnings have to find the prospect first, then make a presentation which, in turn, helps to make the sale. Never, never forget, therefore, that no matter who you are talking to, and whenever you are talking to them, you are making a presentation from the very moment that you open your mouth.

It really does not matter how well you know the person, if you are talking business and if you want to do business, remember the saying 'familiarity breeds contempt'. The better you know your prospect, the more important it is to be polished with your presentation. The better known that prospect is to you, the easier it will be for them to say 'no'. You therefore have to make them want your product or service even more than when you are selling to someone you know less well.

How to Use the Telephone

Let's start at the beginning of the normal sales process. The first thing you have to do is pick up the telephone and speak to somebody. Years of experience in sales has taught me that the average salesperson needs to make fifteen to twenty calls in order to secure an appointment with someone they have never met before. By the end of this week, I shall expect you to have cut those odds down to at least one appointment in five calls. If that does not help you to double your income, I will be amazed.

Now, let's assume that you have the name and telephone number of a potential customer, given to you the previous day by a friend. The first mistake you are likely to make is to assume that you will automatically get an appointment with that person. The very best you can expect is that the mention of your friend's name will get you past the secretary or the person on the switchboard and through to the prospect. Let me emphasize again: your presentation is critical. In any face-to-face meeting you have the advantage of actually being present and therefore acting as a focus and a distraction from what the other person would normally be doing. In addition, you will usually have been expected and time will have been set aside. When your prospect receives a telephone call from you it will probably be unexpected. He or she is likely to be preoccupied with other things, slightly irritated at the interruption and keen to get back to doing what they were doing – which was presumably earning money for them and not you.

Without being there, how do you break that preoccupation, arouse immediate interest and secure the appointment for your full-scale presentation? You cannot impress your prospect with yourself because you are not there. You cannot use visual aids and, worst of all, you don't know which category of buyer he or she falls into. You have only your voice and approximately fifteen seconds, at most.

Put yourself in your prospect's shoes for a moment. What would you like to hear when you accept that incoming call? You would probably want the person calling you to be pleasant and polite and to get straight to the point. You would also like them to be businesslike in their approach, honest about whom they represent and what they are trying to offer you – and to get out of your hair the first time you express a lack of interest.

Your telephone presentation must therefore satisfy and overcome all these points. It must introduce you quickly, arouse interest instantly, pre-empt giving too much information and get you your meeting. Remember that an appointment is all you are trying to sell. The presentation actually to sell your product or service will come later when you are face to face with your prospect.

GETTING THROUGH TO YOUR PROSPECT'S SUBCONSCIOUS MIND

Now let's deal with the above points. Can you be pleasant? Of course you can. If you were actually with your prospect you would be smartly dressed, neatly groomed and would smile when you introduced yourself. In other words, you would create an impression. It is possible to create almost the same impression over the telephone. To do so, and in order to impress the image you wish to impress on your prospect's subconscious, you need to exaggerate everything you would normally do in a face-to-face presentation. If you do not, your own subconscious will work against you and their subconscious will not accept you.

Let me give you two examples to illustrate the point. Some years ago I was asked to do some consultancy work for a company that sold office equipment. The salespeople in this organization worked to a routine pattern. From Monday to Thursday they were out selling. Fridays were spent in the office making appointments for the following week and Saturday mornings were for completing outstanding paperwork.

From Monday to Thursday these salespeople were among the smartest and most well-groomed bunch of professionals you could imagine. Not a hair out of place, not a crease in sight and shoes you could see your face in. On Friday, because all day was spent telephoning prospective clients to arrange appointments, and because there were never any customers visiting the offices, casual dress was accepted practice. Not only was their dress casual. Hair was often untidy, some of the men were unshaven and generally speaking they were a most unattractive group of individuals.

What these salespeople failed to realize was that subconsciously they were projecting precisely this image to their prospective customers. They were naturally sceptical when I explained this to them, but agreed to dress as if they were visiting potential customers when they came in for their next telephone prospecting session. At the end of the following Friday, every single salesperson had filled his or her diary with appointments in less than half the time they normally took. As a bonus, they had also completed their paperwork and had the option of not working on the Saturday morning. Of course, the real champions had made some appointments for the Saturday morning.

Another recent consultancy project I undertook was for a company that rented out pre-recorded video advertising units. To cut down on prospecting time, it employed a team of people to make the appointments for the salespeople. This is not an unusual method in many industries. The company was having a problem with staff turnover and appointment to call ratios, and the salespeople were starting to become very unsettled. My first visit to the telephone sales operation horrified me. People were dressed appallingly. Their desks were littered with plastic coffee-cups, ashtrays were overflowing and the general atmosphere was very unprofessional. On the good side, the staff were all keen, they worked very hard and their telephone script was excellent. They were just not getting the results that were needed.

I explained my theories to the telephone salespeople and asked for their co-operation. We had the offices tidied up, introduced a timetable that allowed six ten-minute coffee breaks a day in addition to the lunch break and banned drinking and smoking at all other times. We gave them the title 'telephone pre-sales executives' and they agreed to dress for work in a businesslike fashion. The men would wear business suits, shirts and ties, the women, skirts and blouses. Anyone who didn't have suitable clothes or the money to buy them was given an interest-free loan.

At the end of the first week under this new regime sales appointments were up 42 per cent. Over the following three years, the company increased its telephone sales force by 25 per cent, was forced to increase its field force by another 60 per cent to cope with the level of appointments being made and is now one of the largest operations of its kind in the United Kingdom.

The reason I illustrate and emphasize these points so strongly is because that first telephone call you make is the most important part of the sales process. Get it wrong and you don't have anybody to sell to; get it right and the sky is the limit.

When you make your telephone calls to potential customers or clients you must be smartly dressed, well groomed and seated at a clean, tidy desk with no coffee-cups or ashtrays in sight. If you would not smoke in front of a non-smoking prospect, don't breathe fumes down the telephone at them. Their subconscious will know you are doing it, and it won't like it.

Smile whenever you would normally smile, but make it a big one. If necessary, have a mirror on your desk and make sure to check that the smile is there at the appropriate time.

Getting Instant Interest

What are you going to say in the few seconds you have that will ensure that you sell your appointment? The most crucial point is that you cannot afford to waste any time. Having established contact you need to introduce yourself and your company. Mention the source of your introduction immediately, and ask politely if you are calling at a convenient time to speak for two minutes. Because you have been polite, you will almost always get the opportunity to speak to your prospect later, if he or she is genuinely busy. More often than not, they will allow you to carry on with your telephone presentation.

Telephone sales techniques tend to fall into two distinct categories. Either you make a statement or you involve the prospect immediately by asking a question. You need planned presentations based on both of these concepts so that you can switch from one to the other as circumstances dictate, always with the aim of arousing interest as quickly as possible. Therefore, when planning a presentation always ask yourself whether, if you were the customer, you would be interested in what you had just said. If the answer is 'no', they won't be either.

Opening Statements Study the following statements carefully. The first in each pair was taken from a company sales script. My comments are in brackets. The second statement in each pair is the better version. Both are opening statements designed to arouse interest. When facts are quoted, they are accurate. There is no point in making claims that will not stand up to scrutiny at a later date.

We sell more engine oil than any other company. [So what? You probably just have more salesmen.]
Seventy per cent of all haulage contractors claim a reduction in servicing costs when they changed to using our engine oil. [That's interesting.]

We have one of the best tennis schools in the area. [That's what they all say.]
We guarantee to improve your game or we refund your fees. [Seems fair – I don't have anything to lose.]

The new version of your sports car is a great improvement on the current model you are driving. [So what? I'm happy with it.]
You'll love the improvements they have made on the new version and the warranty is extended from twelve months to three years. [I loved this

model when I bought it – I wonder what they have done to it. Servicing costs saved would probably cover me in costs if I changed.]

We have one of the best products in the field today. [Who says so?]
The Institute of Architects journal described our product as the best in the industry. [We buy a lot of that item from another company, maybe I should take a look.]

What can you say about your product or service that arouses instant interest? Some of the research you did in Week Two will help you to prepare some versions.

Opening Questions The second way of arousing immediate interest is to ask your prospect a question. Doing this immediately involves them in the presesntation. It always pays to remember that while you are talking the other person has the opportunity to think – and may well be thinking about something other than what you are saying to them. This also applies during a face-to-face meeting, but is even more of a concern when the presentation is being done over the telephone. Always remember that there is a definite reason why we are born with one mouth and two ears. It is simply to remind Psycho-Salespeople that they must spend twice as much time listening as they do speaking. Once your prospect starts to talk he or she stops thinking about anything else and is most likely to give you a clue that will help you get the appointment you need.

Now let's go back to the previous statements and turn these into questions that can involve the prospect and include him or her in the presentation.

Seventy per cent of all haulage contractors using our oil claimed a significant reduction in servicing costs on their fleet. Would you mind telling me how much your servicing bill was in the previous twelve months?

What improvements do you think could be made to improve the standards of coaching at your current tennis school?

Would you mind telling me the features you most enjoyed on the sports car you bought from us last year?

How much credibility do you put on the technical research facilities of the Institute of Architects?

Each of those questions would elicit a response from the prospect that would allow you to follow up with a statement which would almost certainly enable you to raise sufficient further interest to gain the appointment.

Once again, using your own product or service, create a series of questions you can ask that will involve your prospects, arouse further interest and get you the appointments you need to double your income.

Only Sell the Appointment

The biggest trap any salesperson can fall into when prospecting for appointments by telephone is to give away too much information. If you are trying to sell an appointment and have aroused interest, that is the time to close for it. If you allow yourself to be drawn into giving any further information you are in danger of trying to make a telephone presentation of your product or service, a way in which it was not intended to be sold and which you cannot be prepared for.

The easiest way to avoid this trap is simply to say:

Mr Prospect, I cannot possibly give you any further information on the telephone. It would not be fair to either of us. I have something to show you that will save us both a lot of time and will enable you to judge for yourself whether it can be of benefit to you.

With a little alteration, this statement can be applied to almost any product or service I can think of. One salesman I know, whose service just would not fit in with this statement, used it nevertheless. On arrival at his prospect's office, if questioned as to what it was that he had to show, he simply answered, 'Me, sir, and I am the very best person in my field that you are ever going to have the opportunity to do business with.' Maybe that could also be your approach?

Now You Are Face to Face

So now you are in your prospect's office. Everything you say, every move you make, your expressions and your body language, what you are wearing and how you look is critical. You are on stage! Now is the time to put on the performance of your life! However, before you start to make one of the several different presentations you have prepared for your service or product, you want to get as many additional clues as possible to help you decide on the psychological profile of your buyer and therefore which presentation to select.

This is very simple. Most people, be they private buyers, employees in senior positions or partners and owners of companies, all have one common failing which you can exploit to gain the information you require. This goes back to the concept of 'one mouth and two ears'. Some of the most successful men and women I have met spend their lives remembering this. These people rarely speak at length. They say hello then they encourage other people to talk, assimilating information, and storing it away for further use. They study their business contacts in detail. They know the secret I am about to tell you. Almost every prospect's favourite subject is themselves. Your first job, therefore is to get them talking about themselves. How do you do it? Just give them the opportunity. An opening question such as, 'How did you first get into this business?' can turn the fifteen-minute interview you fought for into an hour's dissertation on your prospect's entire history in business. A simple question like, 'Did you start off in this position in the company or have you worked your way up?' will elicit a mass of useful information. In addition, you will probably gather the names of several other people in the company who may well be likely prospects in the future.

Get your prospect talking first. Give him or her the opportunity to supply you with all the information you need to tailor your presentation so that you have the maximum potential for closing the sale.

Selling is all about making someone as enthusiastic about your product as you are. If you are not enthusiastic, you can never expect anyone else to be. However, being over-enthusiastic at the start of your presentation can be almost as bad as having no enthusiasm.

THE 'MATCHING GEARS' TECHNIQUE

There are many Psycho-Sales techniques to make a prospect want to buy your product or service as much as you want to sell it. The first is 'Matching Gears' and should be used as the foundation for any presentation you are making, whatever the buyer's psychological type and no matter what kind of presentation you are giving.

With 'Matching Gears', the objective is to start with a level of enthusiasm that almost exactly matches that of your prospect. Then, using the techniques of mimicry and reverse mimicry which you learned in Week Three, you move your level of enthusiasm up a gear and bring your prospect up to the same level as quickly as you can. If their level of enthusiasm starts to drop back a gear during any part of your presentation, you also drop back a gear. Then change your tack slightly, use the same techniques again to bring them back up and start to accelerate once more.

One of the simplest ways of instantly getting your prospect to move up a gear is to ask a series of short questions at each stage of your presentation. Questions such as 'Does this make sense to you so far?', 'Would that feature increase your office efficiency?', 'Are you with me so far?' and 'Is that an improvement on your existing model?' all involve your prospect and raise his or her level of enthusiasm to match your own. Once they are on your level it is simple for you to accelerate ahead and then bring them up to your level again. At some stage they will be as enthusiastic about your product or service as you could ever be – and you will know the sale is yours for the asking.

THE 'YES FACTOR'

Another, very clever, way of raising someone's level of enthusiasm is by application of the 'Yes Factor'. The psychology behind this is very simple. The more times you can get a prospect to say 'yes' during a presentation, the less likely and the less able they are to say 'no' when you ask for the order. One very successful salesperson I know learned this technique from me and renamed it 'the nodding dog technique'. He rewrote all his sales scripts to incorporate the 'Yes Factor' and his closing ratio increased from one in five appointments to one in two. He obviously more than doubled his income!

The following role play illustrates this technique. You are calling on

Mr Jones. Mr Jones runs a construction company. You have carried out some detailed research on him before your meeting. You think you know his psychological type and you have planned your presentation accordingly.

You: *Good morning. Are you Mr Jones?*
Mr Jones: Yes.
You: *I'm Roger Grant, from Alco Building Supplies. We have an appointment scheduled for 11 a.m. Is there somewhere we can talk privately?*
Mr Jones: Yes. Come this way.
You: *I presume that your friend, Mr Roberts, has telephoned you and told you how satisfied he is with the service that we provide for his company?*
Mr Jones: Yes, he has.
You: *I understand that you have recently relocated to these premises?*
Mr Jones: Yes I have, just a few weeks ago.
You: *And am I right in understanding that you have recently acquired the contract to build seventeen houses on the old Burrows site three miles away?*
Mr Jones: Yes, that's correct. How did you know that?
You: *It's my job to know these things, Mr Jones. I believe that this is one of the largest contracts you have ever undertaken. Is that correct?*
Mr Jones: Yes.
You: *Mr Jones, your previous offices were a long way away from here, weren't they?*
Mr Jones: Yes, they were.
You: *And so are your current suppliers, aren't they?*
Mr Jones: Yes. But they can cope.
You: *And presumably, with this large a project and the need to control cash flow in the early stages, you are going to need small and regular deliveries of materials at very short notice?*
Mr Jones: Yes. That is essential. But my usual suppliers have assured me that they can accommodate me.
You: *That's the XYZ company, isn't it?*
Mr Jones: Yes.
You: *They are on the other side of the motorway, are they not?*
Mr Jones: Yes.

You: *They have also had a series of labour difficulties that have caused delivery problems in the past, haven't they?*

Mr Jones: Yes. But they assure me that those problems are over.

You: *I'm sure they are, Mr Jones. However, human nature being what it is and in today's economic climate, would an absolute guarantee of availability of materials be better for you?*

Mr Jones: Yes, of course it would.

You: *And if those materials could be delivered, or be available within fifteen minutes of placing an order, would that help you keep to schedule and improve your cash flow?*

Mr Jones: Of course it would, but nobody could provide that kind of service, could they?

You: *I'll come on to that Mr Jones. First of all, can you tell me, do you know the exact total quantity of material that you will be using?*

Mr Jones: Yes.

You: *And is there space available on site to accommodate all of this material if it was delivered in one drop?*

Mr Jones: Yes, but you already know that cash flow is critical and we couldn't afford to buy all the materials at one time. What are you getting at?

You: *I'll come on to that. Mr Jones, is it true that if you could afford that level of upfront purchase, you would be able to negotiate a larger discount?*

Mr Jones: Yes.

You: *And there would also be cost savings in terms of unloading materials and distribution of labour on the site, wouldn't there?*

Mr Jones: Yes, there would.

You: *Mr Jones, we are obviously talking the same language. If we were able to place the entire order on site in one go, allow you to draw down stocks as required and stock-check on a weekly basis, and invoice you only for materials that had been drawn down for use, would that be helpful?*

Mr Jones: Yes. Of course it would. But what are your credit terms?

You: *Is that important?*

Mr Jones: Yes, of course it is.

You: *What terms do you get at the moment?*

Mr Jones: Sixty days from delivery.

You: *Is it true to say that you have to keep at least four weeks' additional supplies on site as a safety factor, in case of interruption of supplies or increased needs if you get ahead of schedule?*

Mr Jones: Yes.

You: *So if the materials were on site and you drew them down as you needed them, that would avoid the need for those extra supplies wouldn't it?*

Mr Jones: Yes.

You: *Mr Jones, we can supply the same materials at the same price. We can give you effectively the same credit terms as we can invoice only at the end of each week that you draw down the supplies. You will be in complete control of your project and will save money on the handling of the deliveries. Do we have a deal?*

Mr Jones: Yes, I don't see why not.

Not all sales will go quite as easily as this, but the 'Yes Factor' will make an enormous difference. Mr Jones could have asked many more questions and raised many more objections. The fact of the matter is that because he had said 'yes' so many times, he just could not help but say 'yes' at the first close.

When using the 'Yes Factor', every question has to be phrased to get a 'yes' answer. If you get a 'no' for some reason it is essential to pose at least three other questions which elicit 'yes' responses before asking for the sale.

Follow these rules precisely and you will be amazed at how much more smoothly your sales can progress.

THE POWER OF VISUAL PRESENTATIONS

It is an established scientific fact that people can think much faster than they can speak. There is a well-known saying that 'a picture speaks a thousand words'. Put these together and what do you have? Visual Presentation Material!

Successful companies throughout the world have understood the power of the visual presentation aid and together spend billions of pounds a year producing material for their salespeople. Top salespeople use it and use it well. They earn a lot more money than those who think that they never need an aid to selling.

Let us think about this logically. Whenever you are speaking, the prospect has time to think. He or she can listen and absorb or listen and ignore whatever you are saying. At the same time, because they can think that much faster than you can speak, they have the advantage over you. They can always be one step ahead and you will never know what they are thinking unless they come out with a question.

A visual demonstration of your product or service is one of the most powerful selling aids you can have. Because you are giving your prospect something to focus on, he or she will be kept on track without realizing it. They will also subconsciously try and get ahead of you and anticipate your next step in the sales process, partly out of interest and partly as a defence. A good visual aid will be designed to get your prospect to do this. Without them knowing it, their subconscious will help to sell your product or service to their conscious mind by anticipating the next steps in your presentation.

I shall discuss the use of flattery in your response to objections in the next chapter where we investigate the various methods of handling objections. In the context of a visual presentation, when your prospect successfully anticipates its next stage you have the perfect opportunity to flatter. A praised prospect is inevitably a pleased prospect and a pleased prospect is far more likely to become a customer or client.

VISUAL AIDS AND HOW TO USE THEM

Visual aids come in various forms. The simplest is a single sheet of paper with some graphics and bullet points highlighting the features of your service or product. Then there are desk-top presenters, free-standing presenters, slides, computer-generated displays and, at the top end of the scale, full-colour video presentations.

Visual presentations are wonderful tools to have in your selling kit. However, do not make the mistake of letting them become more important than you. Ultimately, people buy people. It is you that you are primarily selling, and you have to be at the front of the stage. The visual aid, although very important, is just scenery to set the stage and to help to paint the overall picture. It is not a substitute for you. If you are going to use these visual aids, and you certainly should, never let them take the lead role.

I have seen salespeople with stunning personalities who have dramatically reduced their chances of making a sale by putting a desk-top presentation unit between themselves and the person they are selling to, or by seating themselves next to the prospect with the presentation kit in front of both of them. If you cannot maintain eye contact for most of the time that you are using visual material, don't use it. If you feel it is an excellent tool, spend money on having it redesigned so that you stay at the front of the picture whenever you use it.

You may also find that standard, company-produced literature automatically caters for the average buyer or one who is a combination of the conceptual and analytical types. This is another important reason for maintaining control during your presentation. You can emphasize the points that are most relevant to the psychological type of your buyer, and miss out altogether parts of the presentation that appeal to other types. Your prospect will not notice the points that don't appeal to him or her if you don't highlight them. They will notice them if they are forced to go through the whole presentation themselves.

There are three golden rules to remember if you are going to use visual aids successfully.

First, it is essential that you know every single stage of the presentation and can repeat it with your eyes shut and without reference to notes. There is nothing worse than an amateurish visual presentation. Practise it, rehearse it over and over again, and get it right.

Second, your presentation must be flexible and you must involve the prospect at every stage, just as you must in every other type of presentation.

Third, and this is critical, *don't* put away any single piece of your presentation material or kit until you have closed the sale. The moment you start to remove even one piece of material, your prospect will feel that the presentation is over and that he or she is off the hook. Leave the most powerful sheet of your presenter, the last slide on your slide projector or the last frame of your video on-screen in full view while you finalize the sale.

What else do you need to know to make the perfect presentation? Not a lot, other than what you have already learned over the last few weeks. However, you must remember that nothing is ever perfect and that there is always room for improvement.

During the course of this week practise your various and different presentations. Practise them in front of the mirror. Record them, hone them until, finally, they are as razor-sharp as they can possibly be. It is only when they are set in stone in your subconscious that you will be able to present them in a relaxed and professional manner. When you have total confidence in yourself your prospect will have that same level of confidence and will have to buy.

In addition, this week study every piece of visual, promotional material provided to you. Determine how best you can use it and how it can be incorporated in your presentations.

PSYCHO-DYNAMIC EXERCISES

Your relaxation exercises are the same as for last week. In addition, in the evening carry on with your 'power words' exercise. Do not let up on these. You may have already doubled your income or know that you are well on your way to doing so. It does not matter how confident you are, or how certain that you have learned all you need to know – you must carry on with your exercises. If you doubt this, and I doubt that you do, ask your subconscious in one of your quiet moments if you can afford to ease up. However, you already know the answer to that.

Summary of Key Points

● Psycho-Depersonalization can overcome all resistance to cold calling.

● Whoever you are talking to and whenever you are talking to them, you are giving a presentation.

● When telephoning for an appointment, you can arouse a prospect's interest by making a statement or asking a question.

● Almost every prospect's favourite subject is themselves.

● When prospecting by telephone, you must exaggerate what you would normally do in a face-to-face situation.

● Practise the 'Matching Gears' and 'Yes Factor' techniques.

● Prospects think faster than you can speak. Utilize visual aids.

● Practise your presentations until you are word perfect but flexible enough to switch from one to another.

● Carry out your morning and evening exercises.

● Enter your sales records at the end of the week.

WEEK SIX

THE PSYCHOLOGY BEHIND OBJECTIONS AND HOW TO DEAL WITH THEM

When you first set out to double your income five weeks ago, I asked you to carry out your visualization exercises every morning. I asked you to visualize clearly, and in detail, everything that doubling your income could achieve for you. I asked you to imagine all the things you would like to do, the objects you would like to acquire and the places you would like to visit. If you have been doing these exercises correctly you should by now have identified your aims and objectives and be able to picture them down to the minutest detail.

If you want to buy a new house, for example, you should know the precise street in your chosen neighbourhood and have visualized exactly what the house will look like. You should know what it looks like from the outside, the size of its front garden and the flowers and shrubs planted there. You should know the colour of the paintwork and of the brickwork and of the tiles on the roof. Moving to the rear of the house, you should be able to imagine every detail of the landscaped garden. If you want a swimming-pool you should be able to see it and the sunshine glistening on the surface of the water. You should know what types of tree are planted in the garden, be able to visualize the pots and urns of flowers on the patio and know what you will see when you look through the open patio doors that lead from your sun terrace into the living-room.

The inside features of the house should be as real to you as if you already owned it. You should know the colour of the curtains and carpets and be able to see the paintings on the walls and the layout of the furniture. You should even be able to visualize your family living in the house.

If you desire a particular type of car, you should be able to see the colour of the paintwork and of the upholstery and carpet, what the dashboard looks like and the various instruments laid out before you. You will know the size of the engine, its cubic capacity, performance and fuel consumption statistics. You should know the car inside out as if you had owned it for a long time.

If you want to travel and see the world, you should know where you want to go and be able to picture the places clearly. You should be able to visualize them so exactly that you can almost touch them, feel them and smell them.

The beginning of this week is the time to help you stamp these images even more vividly into your subconscious mind.

KEEP A SCRAP-BOOK

When was the last time you kept a scrap-book? Probably not since early childhood. You have heard the expression 'a picture paints a thousand words' and you have clearly defined what it is that you want to achieve. Now you must actually paint the picture. Assuming that very few of you have the artistic ability to do this, the alternative is to start a scrap-book again.

The first thing I want you to do this week is find as many pictures and photographs as possible of precisely what you would like to own, images of what you would like to achieve and pictures and photographs of places you would like to visit. If you have identified the very house you want to buy and know it is currently for sale, go and take a photograph of it, preferably an instant one that you can put into your scrap-book immediately. If you want a particular type of car, go to the showroom and get the most up-to-date brochure – two copies, if necessary, so that you can paste every page into your scrap-book. If seeing the world is your ambition, go to a travel agent and collect brochures on all the places you would like to visit.

Cut out the pictures and paste them into your scrap-book. Whatever it is that you want to own – jewellery, furniture, *objets d'art* – find an illustration for your scrap-book.

Over the next few weeks as you continue with your visualization exercises keep adding new pictures to your scrap-book whenever fresh ideas come into your mind. As a final touch, and to reinforce the message in your subconscious, stick a large self-adhesive label on the front of your scrap-book and, with a broad pen, write clearly on it: 'All this is already mine'.

From now on, carry this scrap-book in your briefcase wherever you go. Whenever you have a spare moment, and particularly before you go in to see a prospect, look quickly through it and remind yourself that every successful sale will bring you that much closer to everything you desire for you and your family.

Never underestimate the power of visualization. The following story is a true one and illustrates this point.

John first came to one of my training sessions two and a half years ago. He told me that during the first few days of carrying out his visualization exercises he had become very confused. It was apparent to him that he did not really know what he wanted. His mind wandered from one thing to another without ever identifying any real objectives. I used a simple analogy to explain to John the importance of identifying his real aims. This may also help you if you have been experiencing any difficulty.

Suppose you live in London and decide to drive to Brighton. You may look at a map first and identify precisely the route you intend to travel. Even if you do not, you will have a good idea of the direction you need to take and, even with some mistakes along the way, you will ultimately arrive. Compare this with getting into your car without knowing where you want to go. You would probably drive around in circles never getting very far from your starting-point. Eventually, with no real destination in view, you would quickly become bored and probably just return home. On your journey to doubling your income it is essential that you have a definite aim and never turn back. If you don't know where you want to go, you will never, ever, get there.

After hearing that analogy John carried out his exercises diligently. Even he was surprised when he identified his real aims and ambitions. Originally, he had no idea of the type of car he wanted to drive or the kind of home he wanted to live in. He had forgotten how much he had enjoyed sailing as a young boy and how much he had loved being in boats. He had certainly never realized that deep in his subconscious was a desire to own an old castle in Tuscany and spend his summer months there among the vineyards.

John has since achieved all of these ambitions. His castle in Tuscany, where I was invited to spend some time last summer, is in one of the most peaceful and idyllic settings I have ever seen.

DON'T BE SURPRISED AT OBJECTIONS

My name is Bruce King, not Martin Luther King, but I too 'had a dream'. It went like this. The chairman and managing director of a major public company visited my offices for a presentation on the marketing campaign we were proposing for them. It was the largest campaign my company had ever pitched for and we would double our income if we won the order. We made our presentation and all the time both the chairman and managing director were nodding and smiling. When we finished they agreed to all our proposals without question, signed the authority for us to commence work, left a large cheque as a deposit and departed. Then I woke up!

No, it did not happen. That type of sale rarely, if ever, does. It is true to say that there is seldom any sale without objections. Why, then, is the average salesperson so surprised when a potential client or customer raises an objection? And why is the average salesperson so often unprepared?

It is very important to understand that handling an objection or a series of objections successfully will ultimately lead to a smooth, easy sale and often eliminate the biggest hurdle that so many average salespeople, and even successful ones, fear: the act of closing. Let's face it: no objections often mean no interest. I cannot think of anything worse than a potential buyer sitting in front of me and saying absolutely nothing. On the other hand, someone who questions, raises objections and has them all answered to their satisfaction has very little to say at the end of a presentation other than 'yes'.

I have heard some sales trainers describe an objection as merely a request for further information. Frankly, I think this is a nonsense. The dictionary definition of objection is 'an expression, statement or feeling of opposition or dislike'. My thesaurus lists the following words as suitable alternatives: censure, counter-argument, doubt, exception, niggle, protest and opposition. How, therefore, could anyone describe an objection as a request for further information? That type of attitude to what is often a genuine initial rejection of your proposals leads to failure to secure an order. Fortunately, the psychology for handling objections is not difficult to understand. There are basically three types of objection: imagined; pretend; and real, or valid.

IMAGINED OBJECTIONS

The imagined objection is just that – a figment of your prospect's imagination. It will inevitably be based on guesswork and a lack of knowledge of the product or service you are going to sell. The following are typical imagined objections which are likely to be unfounded.

I couldn't afford it.
I couldn't afford the running costs of this car, it's probably too heavy on fuel.
I don't know if my wife would like it.
I don't think it would fit.
I don't think this carpet will match my curtains.
I don't think I would be allowed to take that much time off work for this holiday.

Now look at these statements again with my comments in brackets. It will be obvious that these are all imagined objections.

I couldn't afford it. [Your prospect does not know the cost or what credit terms are available.]

I couldn't afford the running costs of this car, it's probably too heavy on fuel. [He or she doesn't yet know that although the engine is larger the new, improved fuel injection system increases fuel economy by 25 per cent.]

I don't know if my wife would like it. [He hasn't asked her yet.]

I don't think it would fit. [He hasn't measured it yet.]

I don't think this carpet will match my curtains. [He or she has not yet seen them together; and, anyway, why not change the curtains at the same time?]

I don't think I would be allowed to take that much time off work for this holiday. [Your prospect hasn't yet asked for it.]

PRETEND OBJECTIONS

What about pretend objections? Probably the most obvious is when a prospect you have just contacted on the telephone claims to be too busy to see you. How many times have you heard that one, and how many times have you failed to overcome it? It is obviously a pretend objection. If I were to telephone and tell you that I had just written a book which would guarantee to double your income in just eight weeks you would almost certainly go out and buy it, wouldn't you? You did, didn't you? Suppose you were to telephone and tell me that you had a proven method that would increase my company's turnover by 40 per cent? If I even half believed you I would make the time to see you, no matter how busy I was. If I could show you a way of reducing the costs of your office administration by 25 per cent, which would mean a saving in excess of £300,000 a year, I am sure you would find fifteen minutes for a meeting at any time of the day or night. If necessary, you would cancel an appointment with someone who didn't have such an attractive benefit to offer. Why then, do you ever believe that someone is genuinely too busy to see you?

Some time ago I telephoned a prospect who had been introduced to me by a very satisfied client. This was in June 1991. The prospect claimed to have far too crowded a schedule, particularly with the expansion of his company's sales operation, and did not feel able to commit himself to an appointment. He asked me to call back in five to six months time. My response went as follows:

Mr Clark, there is a considerable interest in our training programme and I am also very busy. I have my diary in front of me. Could we fix up a meeting for 17 February 1992?

There was a long silence followed by a burst of uncontrollable laughter. I made the appointment for one week ahead. Admittedly, it takes some nerve to do this, but it often works.

Don't be put off by the pretend 'I'm too busy' objection. As a last measure, use the 'Everybody Eats' technique. What do I mean? Mr Fitzpatrick was another potential prospect. He too was too busy to see me for at least three months. Our conversation went along the following lines:

> **Mr Fitzpatrick:** I am far too busy to see you for at least three months.
>
> **Me:** *I can appreciate that, Mr Fitzpatrick. We all have very busy schedules to meet. Can I ask you a question please, Mr Fitzpatrick? Do you eat?*
>
> **Mr Fitzpatrick:** (Pause) Yes, of course I do.
>
> **Me:** *Mr Fitzpatrick, I am happy for you to join me for either breakfast, lunch or dinner, or if necessary all three. Which would be most convenient for you?*

Mr Fitzpatrick joined me for breakfast early one morning and, as a result of that meeting, we secured a major contract with his organization for training their field representatives.

Business on the Menu

To digress for a moment, if you are going to see prospects over a meal there is a golden rule you must adhere to. Over the years, I have spoken to hundreds of salespeople who make a point of entertaining potential customers and clients. So very many of them fall into the same trap. They forget that if you have arranged a business breakfast, lunch or dinner then, between mouthfuls, business is exactly what you should be discussing.

You both know the purpose of your meeting, yet ninety-nine times out of 100 most salespeople forget it completely. They forget to the point that business often is never mentioned during the entire meal and the frustrated salesperson, entirely through his or her own fault, has to resort to making up a follow-up telephone call the next day, or a few days later, to try to secure an appointment to discuss what they wanted to discuss over the meal.

If you are going to spend some of your hard-earned income entertaining prospects in order to make your presentation, put your presentation on the menu. Even before choosing what to eat make it very clear why you wanted to meet the prospect, what you wanted to achieve as a result of the meeting and what you would like to happen afterwards. You cannot possibly carry out a proper presentation with a mouthful of food and a table cluttered with cutlery and plates. But you can make absolutely certain that you will have the opportunity to do so very soon afterwards. Don't miss out! If your prospect has agreed to see you, he or she knows what they are there for. Don't let them down. And don't let yourself down either.

Also, don't forget the art of mimicry. When you do take someone out to breakfast, lunch or dinner, make sure you eat what they eat. The person who has broken bread with you has a bond with you. The person who has broken the same bread with you has a far stronger bond.

Other Pretend Objections

Have you ever been told that it was not within your prospect's budget or that they did not have the authority to make a decision to buy your product or service? In many cases this could be true. However, if you are talking to the owner of a private company, who you know to be the sole decision-maker, this is obviously a pretend objection. In either case you should ask them whether, if it was within their budget or their authority, they would go ahead with the purchase. If the answer is in the affirmative, you are well on your way to making that sale and merely need to provide supporting documentation: your prospect will sell it for you or buy it themselves. If the answer is negative you have not yet established the real objection to your product or service.

Are You Being Tested?

In an earlier chapter I said that people like to deal with experts. Very often a prospect will put forward pretend objections just to test you. He or she will want confirmation that you really know what you are talking about and that you are the type of person they want to establish a business relationship with. You cannot always tell you are being tested from a prospect's posture or tone of voice, and it is therefore important to treat the objection as if it were valid. You are an expert! You are the type of person your prospect would want to deal with. Therefore, deal with the objection objectively. If you are being tested this is your opportunity to prove once and for all that you are precisely the type of person the prospect wants to do business with, and that your product or service is precisely what he or she or their company needs. Whenever a prospect tests you, rise to the occasion. This is your greatest opportunity.

RESPECT IMAGINED AND PRETEND OBJECTIONS

Earlier in the book we discussed the fact that people like to do business with people they like. Among the several attributes you must develop to become a Psycho-Salesperson is the ability to make someone like you and to become their friend. Therefore, the most fundamental principle you must come to terms with when dealing with objections of any kind is never to argue and never to let the experience of handling an objection develop into a confrontation.

The next principle you must accept is that while you may know that an objection is either imagined or pretend you must always treat it as if it were valid. Nobody likes to be ignored and dealing with every type of objection as if it were a valid one will gain you the respect and friendship of your prospect – who will be willing for you to continue with your sales presentation.

Imagined or pretend objections are very easy to overcome when dealt with as if they are valid. They are generally raised near the beginning of your presentation and it is essential that you deal with them professionally and efficiently. This will not, however, guarantee your sale. Valid objections will follow the imagined and pretend ones – and these are really important.

VALID OBJECTIONS

Having spent many years teaching hundreds of people to sell a huge variety of products and services, it has become apparent to me that the objections that can be raised against any product or service may differ but there are never more than six valid ones. We have already established that if you can deal with objections successfully a sale will almost always result. It is therefore essential to know the objections that can be levelled against what you are selling, and to practise and rehearse different answers to them. Each answer must be tailored to the type of objection that is likely to be raised by the different types of buyer.

The Six Valid Objections

The following, very different, examples illustrate my point that six is the maximum number of valid objections that can be raised against any product or service. Let us take life insurance, probably the ultimate in conceptual sales, first. There is no other product or service where the purchaser cannot possibly receive any personal benefit whatsoever from its acquisition other, perhaps, than a coffin. As with the sale of most products, your presentation and the way you handle objections must be prepared differently for analytical and conceptual buyers. Unlike most product sales, it is possible for the prospect to raise during the presentation a number of objections which to you may seem to be mainly imagined objections. Never forget, however, that an imagined objection that is perceived to be valid by the prospect must be treated as valid by the salesperson.

The six major perceived valid objections that can be raised during a life insurance presentation are:

1 I don't agree with it.
2 I can't afford it.
3 I have got enough.
4 I'm too old.
5 I don't care what happens when I am dead.
6 I do not need any.

It does not matter whether the prospect is analytical or conceptual or which of the sub-categories they come within. With very few exceptions, these are the objections they raise.

Now let us take a product which should appeal most to an analytical buyer, but which must also be sold to a conceptual one: an automated hot-drinks machine for the office. The six major valid objections, one or more of which is likely to be raised during a presentation, are:

1 We do not want one.
2 We do not need one.
3 We already have one.
4 They are too expensive to run.
5 We cannot afford one.
6 We do not like the quality of machine made coffee.

I doubt that any other objections could be raised that are not obviously either imagined or pretend ones.

PSYCHO-RULES

These are the basic techniques for handling all objections – imagined, pretend and valid.

PSYCHO-RULE NUMBER ONE

Let them finish!

We have already discussed the fact that nobody likes to be ignored. Neither do they like to be interrupted. If you really want to handle objections properly, you will want your prospect to give you as much information as possible. Therefore, don't interrupt them when they start to object. Hear them out and take careful note mentally or, if appropriate, in writing, of what precisely the objection is. You cannot answer it properly without the full information. If you interrupt you will immediately alienate your prospect. It really does not matter how many times you have heard the objection before, and how easily you can answer it, you can only score points by listening all over again.

PSYCHO-RULE NUMBER TWO

Ask your prospect to elaborate on the objection

Even if you fully understand it and know what to answer – don't! Simple questions such as 'How do you mean?', or 'I am not sure that I understand that question, can you elaborate please?', can elicit a great deal of useful information. For the conceptual buyer, questions such as 'Why do you feel that way?' or for the analytical buyer, 'How do you work that out?' will provide you with valuable information that will enable you to continue with a successful presentation.

The other major advantage in asking a prospect to elaborate on an objection is that in many cases he or she will talk themselves out of it without you having to say anything. This is particularly true of the imagined or pretend objection. Many times I have thrown one of these back to my prospect and, after a lengthy silence and possibly some waffled explanation, he or she has agreed, without any prompting from me, that the objection was in fact invalid.

PSYCHO-RULE NUMBER THREE

If the objection is a valid one you can deal with it either immediately or later

If you feel that the rest of your presentation, structured in the way you like to present it, will deal with the objection, ask your prospect if you can discuss it later – and make sure you do. If it is a stumbling-block, deal with it immediately.

PSYCHO-RULE NUMBER FOUR

Get it out of the way

Once you have answered an objection it is absolutely essential that you get your prospect's agreement that it no longer exists. Do not assume that because you have answered it to your satisfaction you have answered it to his or hers. Ask 'Have I covered that to your satisfaction?' or 'Are you now satisfied completely on that point?' or 'Is there anything else you need to know on that subject before I continue?' Getting your prospect's confirmation that the objection no longer exists removes the likelihood of their subconscious raising it again when you are asking for the sale. An objection that has not been satisfactorily answered, and confirmed as irrelevant by your prospect, can always be brought up at a later stage taking you right back to the beginning of your presentation. By then, you may have run out of time.

Let us remind ourselves again of the two main types of buyer and their sub-categories: the analytical buyer and the conceptual buyer and, in each case, the grumpy, the friendly, the timid, the procrastinator, the snob and the dealer. The same Psycho-Rules apply in every single case but the subtle differences in your handling of each of the two main categories and various sub-categories will have a dramatic impact on your sales success.

ANALYSE OBJECTIONS AND TAILOR YOUR ANSWERS TO THEM

Your task now is to sit down quietly and list every possible objection you can think of that could be raised, or has been raised, when you are presenting your product or service. Divide a large sheet of paper into three separate columns labelled 'Imagined', 'Pretend' and 'Valid' and put the objections in the relevant column. If necessary, put some of them into more than one column. Next, take a separate sheet of paper and head it 'The Analytical Buyer', then divide it into columns – one for each sub-category of buyer. Write the sub-category at the top of each column. Do same on a separate sheet of paper headed 'The Conceptual Buyer'. If necessary, duplicate these sheets so that you have several copies of each.

Now I want you to take each and every objection you have listed and prepare a polite, sensible and objective answer to each one. Remember that the approach to each of your two main types of buyer is totally different, as is the way you handle the sub-categories. Write your answers in the relevant columns on both sheets of paper.

If necessary, before completing your responses go back to Week Three and review the psychological profiles of buyers in the various sub-categories and how they need to be spoken to. Choose your words with infinite care basing them on these profiles and you will have the key to handling the objections. When you have completed this, practise and rehearse until you can answer any objections.

PAUSE, THINK, RESPOND

Before you answer an objection always remember the 'Pause, Think, Response' technique. It means just that and if you don't use it your handling of objections will have a fraction of the impact it could otherwise have.

First, before responding to any objection: *pause*. Even if you automatically know the answer to it don't immediately blurt it out. Whether it is an imagined, pretend or valid objection, your prospect needs to know you are taking it seriously. By pausing as if to think about it, you give the impression that you are giving it careful thought and consideration before replying. Use the time to *think*. Your *response* must reflect this care and consideration and your choice of words must depend on the psychological profile of your prospect.

Your Opening Line

You need to have a very good opening statement and, ideally, several that can be used for each type of prospect. For example, Mr Grumpy would be most impressed if your response to his objection started with sympathetic agreement. The words 'I absolutely agree, Mr Grumpy, however, have you considered . . .' would be appreciated by someone like him. He needs sympathy and agreement before you reinforce your original statement. Mr Timid, who is scared of making decisions and with whom you need to take your presentation very slowly, will appreciate an opening statement such as, 'That's a very valid point, Mr Timid. I am probably going much too fast and I apologize. Have you considered the possibility . . .?' Mr Friendly, Mr Procrastinator, Mr Snob and Mr Dealer will all respond to opening statements such as, 'That's a very good point, however . . .'; 'That's a very interesting observation, however . . .'; 'That's a very important point and I'm glad you raised it, however . . .'

In every one of those statements you are flattering the prospects and appealing to their basic psychological profiles and subconscious minds. As a result, your response will be taken as coming from a genuine, concerned and caring salesperson.

Follow this technique and you will find each and every objection ever easier to deal with.

DON'T WASTE YOUR TIME

There is a technique you should not employ, yet which many salespeople fail to resist. It is called the 'Banging Your Head Against a Brick Wall' technique. In other words, there are sometimes genuine reasons why your prospect cannot have any use for your product or service and will not buy it. You will remember that in Week Four we discussed the fact that you cannot sell running-shoes to someone with no legs or a radio to a deaf person. If you are listening to your prospect, and have not lost your hearing, there will be occasions when you will realize that, despite your careful research before your initial approach, you have got it wrong and there is a genuine reason why that person cannot buy from you.

If your product requires finance and your prospect has a zero credit rating because of problems with their business there is no point in continuing with your presentation. If he or she has recently lost their driving licence there is very little point in trying to sell them a car. There are many other examples yet, time after time, salespeople continue to push forward with their presentation knowing full well that there is no possibility of making a sale.

Time is your most valuable asset – don't waste it! If you know that your prospect has no need for your product, or does not have the ability to buy it, bow out gracefully – but not before asking whether he or she knows anybody else who might be interested in and need what you have been presenting. This is just another example of a Win-Win situation. Your prospect has no time to waste listening to a presentation; and you, by acknowledging the impossibility of the situation, may just win a few qualified, referred leads by accepting it.

TAKE A REFRESHER

The dream I mentioned in the early part of this chapter was a good one. I have also had a few bad dreams. These have not necessarily taken place at night while I was asleep. Sometimes they are a very real part of my, and any other Psycho-Salesperson's, working day.

Sometimes, often when you least expect it, everything starts to go wrong. Your sales figures plummet, your confidence falls from an all-time high to an all-time low and in just the space of a few hours you feel that nothing will ever go right again.

It is not always entirely your fault. The economy or your prospect's circumstances can change. Some markets are constantly shrinking while others are expanding and each can take their turn. However, another reason can be that when you start to fly high it is very easy to forget some of the most basic principles that earned you money in the past and which you are failing to use now. This can happen over a matter of days, weeks, months or years. Don't let this happen to you.

If you think you may have forgotten any part of this book, or if there is anything you have learned so far that you are not using to its fullest extent in your quest to double your income, just take an evening off from bowling, the cinema or whatever else it is that you are doing in your social life, and re-read the first few chapters. It never does any harm to be reminded or to take a refresher course. A quick swim in an ice-cold pool of water after a hot sauna can get every nerve and muscle tingling throughout your system. A quick dip back through the first few chapters of this book can remind and revitalize you, and make all the difference to your sales figures this week.

WE DO IT BECAUSE WE LOVE TO – NOT BECAUSE WE HAVE TO

As if you had not had enough excitement for one week, here's one more thing to think about: 'Psycho-Salespeople do it because they love it – not because they have to do it.' By now you should be more than half-way to doubling your income – in just a few short weeks. By practising the techniques you have learned so far, and those that you will learn in the remaining chapters, you will have the opportunity to double your income, and double it again. Psycho-Salespeople never have to worry about money. They are amongst the top 5 per cent of earners in any country. They work because they want to, not because they have to. They maintain that high level of income and that high standard of living because it just happens naturally. They do not have to work – but they love to work! If you re-read every chapter you've read so far and go out every day this week practising the techniques for prospecting, presenting and handling objections that you have learned up to now, you must make a lot more money. However, I am going to ask you to – **take a day off work**!

Go out with a friend or your family and enjoy yourself. Talk light-heartedly, about what you have learned and what it is doing for you now and will do in the future. Spend a little of the money you have worked so hard for in the last few weeks and enjoy yourself. It will not be time wasted – it will be time well spent.

PSYCHO-DYNAMIC EXERCISES

Every day this week, including the day that you take off, practise your morning relaxation exercises and Psycho-Dynamic visualization processes. Have a good look through your scrap-book and see what things in it are already yours. Every evening, after your relaxation exercises, practise your power word associations. Complete your sales records at the end of the week and accept my congratulations now. You are doing a great job!

Summary of Key Points

● Buy a scrap-book and paste in pictures of all the things you want to own and all the places you want to visit. Look at it before every sales presentation.

● Without objections, there is rarely any interest.

● There are three types of objections: imagined, pretend and valid. All three must be treated as valid.

● If you have a business breakfast, lunch or dinner – business must be on the menu.

● There are only six valid objections that can be raised against your product or service. Identify them and make sure you have an answer tailored to each psychological type of buyer.

● There are four major psycho-rules for dealing with objections effectively. Learn them.

● Take a day off – you've earned it.

● Practise your daily exercises.

● Enter your sales figures at the end of the week.

WEEK SEVEN

CLOSE THAT SALE
PSYCHO-CLOSES
THAT GUARANTEE
SALES SUCCESS

ASK FOR THE ORDER

Salespeople don't plan to fail but they often fail to close. This point was vividly illustrated to me some years ago by a shower salesman. My family and I had recently moved to a very expensive neighbourhood. We had chosen a slightly smaller house than we really needed because of the high prices in the area.

We decided to install a shower-room to ease the morning queue outside the bathroom.

A representative from a well-known company visited us late one afternoon. He was very presentable and knew his product well. I was impressed. He spent the first half an hour running through the various models that were available and the technical specifications of each. I mentally decided on the most appropriate one for our needs. After a tour of inspection of the house, and after taking measurements in various rooms, the most appropriate site in which to install the equipment soon became very apparent. Over a cup of coffee we ran through the technical specifications of the model I had already set my mind on and the costs of supply, delivery and installation. I was ready to sign the order. At this point, this super-salesman thanked us for our time and patience, left a pile of literature on our coffee-table, and got up and left. His parting words were, 'I'll wait to hear from you then.'

I was totally flabbergasted. I wanted the equipment. I wanted to buy it from his company and I was ready to sign an order form immediately. He did not ask me to. His lack of enthusiasm to close the sale of the shower actually rubbed off on me and the following day over breakfast my wife and I decided that we could probably do without the equipment anyway as it was very likely that we would be moving on again in a year or so.

You may think this is an extreme example, but I can assure you that thousands of times every day, in every country throughout the world, a salesperson fails to ask for the order. Even when there is an obviously willing buyer and an apparently willing seller, and where the sale is there for the asking, the same old rule applies. If you don't ask for it – you don't get it!

You Owe It to Your Customer

If somebody walks into your shop or showroom, or if a prospect agrees to see you, they must be interested. Nobody is ever, really, just look- ing. If you know there is a need for your product or service, and that the money is available to buy it, you owe it to your prospect to get the sale over and done with as quickly and smoothly as possible. It is just as difficult for them to make the buying decision as it is for the average salesperson to attempt to close the sale. The Psycho-Salesperson has no such problem. He or she knows that the prospect needs it, the pros- pect can afford it and the prospect probably wants it. Their job is to make that buying decision as simple and painless as possible.

IF YOU DON'T ASK – YOU DON'T GET

Why is it that the word 'close' seems to strike such terror into the hearts and minds of even the most experienced and competent salespeople. If it is the right prospect with the need and the means to buy, if the presentation has run smoothly and objections have been handled successfully, asking for the order should be the natural and obvious ending to the meeting. So often it just does not happen.

A few years ago a briefcase manufacturer introduced a novel product called The Recording Briefcase on to the market. It was one of the company's standard models but incorporated within the locking mechanism was a high-frequency tape-recorder and microphone that could record conversations up to one and a half hours long.

The launch of this product coincided with a project my consultancy was undertaking for a company who manufactured and sold a range of cosmetics and toiletries to pharmacists and supermarkets throughout the United Kingdom. They were rapidly losing their market share in spite of an excellent product range and we had been called in to identify the problem within the sales force and to design new training schedules for their salespeople if necessary.

We decided to provide some of the sales force with the recording briefcases and asked them to record their sales interviews throughout the day for a two-week period. The results were staggering. Out of a team of forty-five people selected for the trial, 25 per cent never asked a closing question. They made their presentation and then waited for the buyer to give them an order. If the buyer did not offer one, they did not ask for one. By contrast, all the top salespeople in the group, who were responsible for over 80 per cent of the sales during the trial period, attempted to close at least five times before giving up. Those results spoke for themselves.

We followed up with more detailed research involving the entire sales force of 325 people. The results were equally staggering. The average salesperson knew only two closes or two different ways of asking for an order.

How could they possibly expect to achieve the targets the company had set for them or that they had set for themselves?

The target you have set for yourself is to double your income in just eight weeks. If you only knew two or three ways of closing a sale up to now, you will know a dozen or more tried, tested and proven ways of helping you achieve your targets by the time you have read this chapter.

WHEN DO YOU CLOSE?

Salespeople who attend my courses often ask me when precisely they should start closing. My answer is very simple: you are starting to close from the first moment that you open your mouth.

This is no exaggeration. There are obviously times when you should try and close a sale immediately rather than continue with your presentation. Study your prospect carefully and he or she will give you very clear indications of just when to do this. These are some of the more obvious signals they will send to you.

Buying Signals

The prospect who smokes cigarettes may not have done so earlier in your presentation or may have smoked a little. If he or she suddenly lights a cigarette when you least expect it, and their attitude changes even slightly, you know that the time is right. If anything about the pace of their behaviour changes, whether it quickens or slows down, you have reached a point in your presentation where their interest is heightened to the point of being ready to buy. Try a close and see how they react. Don't go past that point in your presentation and let the opportunity slip.

If your prospect suddenly starts nodding and smiling they are ready for a close. If their body language changes for the better they are ready for a close. If they start asking a lot of questions about the least important benefits of your product or service, you know they have already bought the major ones. They are ready to be closed right then. Don't lose another second – they are waiting for you to help them make the decision. In other words, whenever your prospect's subconscious mind takes over from his or her conscious mind, your Psycho-Sales techniques have won the day and it is time to write up your order.

PSYCHO-CLOSES – WHAT YOU'VE BEEN WAITING FOR

In the last six weeks you have learned some of the most powerful techniques for prospecting, presenting your product or service and handling objections and turning them into sales opportunities. You have programmed your subconscious mind to be able to utilize these techniques as if they were second nature to you. Now is the time for you to learn some of the most powerful closes used by successful Psycho-Salespeople and to put some of the finishing touches to what is about to become one of the most successful selling machines in the world today: you.

PSYCHO-CLOSE ONE
Closing on the Real Objection
No prospect will ever give the real objection to buying your product or service the first time you try to close. In most cases, they themselves don't really know what it is. It is your job to help them identify it. Several phrases can be used to help the prospect, and you, define precisely what the real objection is.

The following role play illustrates these:

Salesperson: *Mr Prospect, this piece of equipment meets all of the technical specifications and requirements that you laid down. If you would like to sign the order form here, I can have it delivered to you by the end of the week.*
Prospect: I'm not sure that I can afford it.
Salesperson: *Just suppose that the cost was not a problem Mr Prospect. Is there any other reason for you not wanting to place an order right now?*
Prospect: I am not certain that any of the colours it is available in will fit in with the colour scheme in our living-room.

Salesperson: *In addition to that Mr Prospect, is there anything else at all that is concerning you?*

Prospect: Well, to be perfectly honest with you, I am not sure that my wife will like it.

Salesperson: *Mr Prospect, your wife is going to love this and it will be a lovely surprise. Over 85 per cent of these units are purchased for the home by women and this model in pale cream will fit in with any decor. You need have no worries about surprising your wife with this unit. If you would just like to authorize the order here, I will have it gift-wrapped and delivered. What time is most convenient for our delivery man to call?*

In this example, you can see that the prospect was not concerned about the price or the colour. Those objections did not even require an answer. His sole concern was whether or not his wife would like it – and that was easily dealt with.

The worst mistake a salesperson can make is always to take the very first objection that is raised and settle that to the prospect's satisfaction before moving on. In many cases the potential buyer will just come up with one time-wasting objection after another. To answer some of them you may even have to go away and return with satisfactory evidence which, at the end of the day, wasn't really required in the first place. Why drag a sale out over three to four weeks when, by establishing the real objection, it can be closed immediately?

Let's take another example:

Salesperson: *Mr Prospect, this van is in the precise price range that you indicated to me, has the same carrying capacity as your existing fleet and we can have your company logo painted on the sides and delivered to you this week. If you would just like to OK this order form right here, we can get on with the work.*

Prospect: I am still concerned. I know that the van can carry the same volume as the model we are already using, but I am not so sure that with the smaller wheels it will be able to carry the weight of some of our loads.

Salesperson: *I understand your concern. I have the technical data available that can prove to you that this would be no problem. However, in addition to that, is there anything else that is preventing you from placing the order?*

Prospect: The engine is also a little smaller. Won't we have to service this at slightly more regular intervals?

Salesperson: *Suppose that was not a problem Mr Prospect, is there anything else at all that is worrying you?*

Prospect: Well, to be absolutely frank with you, I cannot afford to go ahead right now. We are a little tight on our budget and I don't think we could manage to pay for it until the next quarter, at the very earliest.

Salesperson: *I think we can help you with that as well. If I were able to arrange for you to pay 20 per cent deposit now and spread the balance of the payments over the next three quarters, would you be in a position to sign the order right now?*

Prospect: That would certainly help.

Salesperson: *Here's the data on the weight-carrying capacity and servicing schedule, which you see is, in fact, an improvement on your existing model. If you would like to OK the order just here, I will have the finance director bring down the paperwork for the payment schedule.*

Prospect: Thank you.

In this example, the prospect's queries about the volume capacity and servicing schedules were, in fact, stalls. The real problem was the finance. Our salesperson nevertheless answered the queries on the technical specification, but only after dealing effectively with the major objection.

Spend as much time as necessary and ask as many questions as you have to until you identify the real, final objection. By doing so you will more than double your chances of closing the sale.

PSYCHO-CLOSE TWO

The Power of Silence

Anybody who saw Alfred Hitchcock's *Psycho* will remember how the tension increased during the long silent periods in various scenes. In many thrillers silence is used to build up tension and inevitably has people sitting on the edge of their seats. There is no power like the power of silence and this applies equally in any sales situation.

The golden rule is: whenever you ask a closing question, shut up. The first person to speak will almost certainly be the loser. If it is your prospect, he or she either has to say 'yes' to your proposition or raise another objection to going ahead. It will almost certainly be an objection that you can deal with and your prospect will be on the defensive again. If you speak first, the prospect is off the hook and you are in the defensive position and will have to spend a lot more time trying to regain control of the situation.

Charles was an ex-fighter pilot who had taken early retirement. He went to work for a company who specialized in leasing executive jets to large corporations and attended one of my training courses where he learned of the power of silence. Some months later he recounted this story to me.

Charles had been negotiating with the chairman and chief executive of a well-known public company for some weeks. The meetings had not gone terribly well but Charles managed to persuade them to take a trial flight in the jet he proposed to lease them. He hoped that a demonstration of the speed and efficiency of the service would convince them of its value to their company. He hired a chauffeur-driven limousine, collected the chairman and chief executive from their office and drove them to the private section of the airfield where they embarked for their trial flight.

Charles was not happy with the way things went. His prospects were very quiet during the entire flight and, in spite of several probing questions, he could elicit little response. His prospects exchanged a few whispered words during the flight and, from time to time, made a few notes in their diaries. At the end of the flight they disembarked and got back into the limousine, which was waiting on the tarmac for them, for their journey back to their office.

Charles sat facing them in the rear of the car on the homeward journey and once again, although he made several attempts to strike up a conversation, his prospects remained silent throughout almost the entire journey.

As the car drew into the dimly lit underground car-park beneath his prospects' office Charles felt considerably less than confident. He was almost certain that once his prospects were out of the car he would never see them again. As the car drew to a halt, he made his move. 'Gentlemen', he said, 'in our earlier meetings, I believe I answered all your questions to your entire satisfaction. The trial flight that you have experienced has demonstrated beyond doubt that the efficiency and cost-effectiveness of this service would be of immense benefit to your company.'

Charles then withdrew a contract and a pen from his inside jacket pocket, placed it on the small table between the seats and said: 'If you would just sign this authority for us to proceed, we can have the jet ready for your use by the end of this week.' He then sat back, smiled and kept quiet. Neither the chairman nor the chief executive smiled back. This took place at precisely 4.10 p.m. Sitting there in the silence of that dimly lit underground car-park, every minute seemed like an hour to Charles. At 4.22 p.m. the chairman picked up the contract and the pen, smiled and signed.

Charles earned more money in that twelve minutes of silence than he had earned in his last twelve months as a Royal Air Force pilot.

The next time you ask a prospect a closing question remember Charles: keep quiet and you keep control. There is no close more powerful than The Silent Close.

The rules should almost never be broken. However, for those bold and impatient enough to try it, the power of silence can occasionally be broken by the 'Confucius Close'.

The 'Confucius Close' is simply a way of bringing the silence to an end without losing too much impact. After a few minutes silence, or as much as you can take or have the patience for, turn to your prospect and say: 'Confucius say, silence means agreement.' This must be said quietly, with extreme confidence and with a genuine smile.

It is taking your life in your hands but, done properly, will almost always work.

PSYCHO-CLOSE THREE

Turning a Question Into a Sale

This is another very powerful closing technique and there are frequent opportunities to use it during most sales presentations.

How can you turn a question from a prospect into a close? Let's look at a few examples:

Prospect: Does it come in red?
Salesperson: *Would you like it in red?*
Prospect: Yes. [They've bought it.]

Prospect: Is there a diesel version?
Salesperson: *Would you like a diesel version?*
Prospect: Yes. [They've bought it.]
Prospect: Can I pay for this monthly?
Salesperson: *Would you like to pay for it monthly?*
Prospect: Yes. [They've bought it.]
Prospect: Do they make it in a larger size?
Salesperson: *Would you like it in a larger size?*
Prospect: Yes. [They've bought it.]

Simple, isn't it? And yet some salespeople even manage to ruin this one. The salesperson's attitude and choice of words is vital. The following example is a classic case of how not to do it:

Prospect: Is there a diesel version of this model?
Salesperson: *If there is a diesel model available, will you buy it?*
Prospect: No. [They haven't bought it.]

Turning a question into a sale will work wonders for your closing ratios and, with practice, can be introduced many times into any presentation. It can also be sharpened up, depending on the type of question you are asked. For example:

Prospect: Is this model available in a diesel version?
Salesperson: *Would you like it in a diesel version?*
Prospect: Possibly. Would it be available by the end of the following week?
Salesperson: *If I can get it to you before then, are you prepared to approve the order today?*
Prospect: Yes. [They've bought it.]

PSYCHO-CLOSE FOUR

Starting the Presentation with a Close

A really sharp Psycho-Salesperson can start a presentation with a close. I once worked for a major United Kingdom life insurance company. Prospecting for potential clients is often very difficult in the insurance industry and in many cases salespeople I knew had to make fifty to sixty telephone calls to secure an appointment. Having done so, they would arrive at the prospect's place of work or home and go into a lengthy presentation about themselves and their company. They would then carry out what is known as a 'fact find' to determine which of their products was most likely to be suitable for the prospect. Inevitably this would lead to a two- or three-visit sale.

I decided to find the magic sentence that could reduce these visits to one and, in addition, reduce the amount of time spent on each call.

Bearing in mind how difficult it was for most salespeople to get in front of a client, the answer soon became obvious. At my very next appointment, once I had introduced myself and exchanged the normal brief courtesies, I asked the prospect the following question: 'Mr Prospect, I am sure you get a lot of calls from companies like ourselves over the course of the year. In view of the fact that you agreed to see me, was there anything in particular that you needed to discuss?' I was amazed at the result. Without any prompting from me, my prospect told me exactly what he wanted and how much he was prepared to spend on it. This was repeated in approximately 50 per cent of the visits I made. That simple, magic sentence halved the time I spent with most prospects and, as a result, allowed me to treble my sales in a relatively short space of time.

Prospects often don't really know what they want until a direct question makes them think about it. A very successful car salesman I know asks the same opening question of every person who walks into his showroom. It is simply: 'Good morning sir (or madam), are you here today to buy a car?' He has doubled his sales using this sentence. When confronted with this question, people who had entered his showroom thinking they were just looking suddenly realized precisely what they were there for: they did actually want to buy a new car.

How can this be applied to your product or service? Do you work in a furniture store? If someone walks over and examines a three-piece suite, how about saying: 'Good morning madam, are you here today to buy a three-piece suite?' Nothing ventured, nothing gained. If the prospect says 'no', you are no worse off than when you started.

Here is another example. A Unit Trust salesman I knew used to start his interview with the statement: 'If I could show you the best possible investment, how much would you have to invest?' No matter what the prospect replied, the salesman repeated the question until he got an answer. Once he had established the size of the investment he was straight into his presentation. The close had already been done.

Some products or services can rarely be sold this way, but keep this particular close in mind. On the occasions when it can be used it can produce very dramatic results.

PSYCHO-CLOSE FIVE

The Balance Sheet Close

The Balance Sheet Close is particularly useful when dealing with procrastinators and timid and grumpy buyers, whether they are analytical or conceptual.

They all tend to have difficulty in raising objections and find it just as difficult to make decisions. The Balance Sheet Close is an excellent way of forcing a decision.

If you are going to use this type of close it is very important that you practise it over and over again until you become fluent and professional in your presentation.

Your script should be based on the following:

Mr Prospect, I appreciate how difficult it can sometimes be to make a decision. Many people, and particularly those in more senior positions, have so much on their minds that they have developed a decision-making procedure which saves them a lot of time and, ultimately, a lot of money. This was demonstrated to me some years ago, Mr Prospect, by the chairman of a major public company, who informed me that as a result of using this formula he had saved and made his company many millions of pounds. I am sure this will be very helpful to you with our current situation. May I explain to you what we need to do?
[Prospect: Yes please.]
We will take this large sheet of paper, Mr Prospect, and divide it into two columns. On the left-hand side we will head the column 'Reasons for going ahead now'. (Take the emphasis off the word 'now' as you speak it but make sure that you write it in slightly larger letters.)

At the top of the other column we will write 'Reasons for not going ahead now'. (This time you emphasize the word 'now'.)

The next thing we do is to put down all of the reasons for making a positive decision in this left-hand column and then the reasons against in the right-hand column. When we have finished, if there is a significant difference between the numbers in either of the two columns, then the decision will be made for us, Mr Prospect, don't you agree? (Without waiting for confirmation of this, continue:) *Mr Prospect, what are some of the positive points that we have discussed so far?*

From now on you prompt your prospect as much as possible, give him suggestions and write in the left-hand column as many definite reasons for going ahead as you possibly can. If you have prepared yourself thoroughly beforehand you should be able to get down at least thirty to forty good reasons why your prospect should go ahead with the purchase right now. When you have done this, push the piece of paper across to your prospect, hand over your pen and ask him to write in the right-hand column as many reasons as he can for not going ahead now. The difference is that this time you offer him absolutely no help whatsoever.

Remember that there is probably a maximum of only six valid objections that can be raised about your product and probably no more than three or four imagined or pretend ones, most of which you will have dealt with by now.

I have never yet met a prospect who managed to get down more than four or five reasons against going ahead with my proposals when faced with the Balance Sheet Close. When your prospect has finished writing, or when you see that he is having a problem, simply lean across the desk or table, look at the sheet, look him in the eyes and say: 'Mr Prospect, that seems to have made our decision for us, doesn't it?'. Then go smoothly into your closing sequence.

I was once selling to a Mr Timid who was probably one of the worst examples of his psychological type that I have ever come across. If it had not been for the fact that the sale was ultimately worth in excess of £35 000 in commission to me, I don't think I would have had the patience to continue.

After my first attempt at a close Mr Timid had five reasons against going ahead with the sale. Together we had written down over thirty-five reasons for going ahead. He still would not make a decision. Twenty-five minutes later we had our 'Reasons for' column up to a total of fifty-five and had increased the 'against' list by only one. Mr Timid still would not make a decision.

Twenty minutes later we had reached the grand total of eighty-two 'Reasons for', running on to five sheets of paper. Mr Timid was stuck at six and agreed the sale.

Most types of analytical buyer will work with you on the Balance Sheet Close if you present it properly in the first place. If you stick with it the time and effort involved will almost always be justified.

PSYCHO-CLOSE SIX

The Maybe You Cannot Afford It Close

This close is absolutely made for the snob and the dealer, whether analytical or conceptual. It appeals to their most basic instinct – their sense of pride.

To make this close work successfully you need to underplay your hand. Confrontation or an outright challenge will work entirely against you if you are not careful.

The Maybe You Cannot Afford It Close can be used whenever you are selling more than one of a particular item and where superior and more expensive versions of your products are available that will earn you more money.

It can also be used for any service that can be offered at different levels at different costs and for any programme or system where installation is normally carried out over a period of time in order to spread the costs for the client.

A real estate developer in California who learned this technique from me used it very successfully when a development of 142 condominiums that he had up for sale along the coast were not selling too well. I suggested that he might promote them as investments for holiday rentals, as opposed to permanent homes, and the market at the time seemed right to take this suggestion forward.

A typical Mr Snob visited the development sales office one morning and my client informed him that although units were available singly there were substantial discounts on multiples of five or more. In a soft voice he added the words, 'although I don't suppose that's within your budget, is it?' This was done very politely and with very little emphasis but Mr Snob rose to the bait. 'Of course I can afford five units,' he said. 'Where do I sign?'

We found out later that Mr Snob had a rather difficult time talking his bank manager into lending him the money, but his sense of pride and vanity couldn't cope with being told he couldn't afford the purchase. He had to go out of his way to prove that he could.

I personally have used this close on many occasions with great success. In preparing a financial planning programme for a potential client it is quite common to put together one which, under normal circumstances, would generally be put into place over a two- to four-year period.

A Mr Snob or a Mr Dealer can be persuaded to close immediately. The words I used with these buyers were:

I have put these proposals together for you and I am sure you will find them very interesting. They will help you to achieve precisely the objectives you have given to me. However, in view of the complexity and cost, I don't suppose that you will be able to afford to effect all the contracts today and, therefore, I think we need to look at a planned process of installation over the next two to three years.

I knew that Mr Snob or Mr Dealer would automatically rise to the bait. Without this challenging approach, he would have suggested a two- to three-year plan himself. On the basis of my challenge to his subconscious all the transactions were invariably carried out immediately.

Whenever you come across a Mr Snob or a Mr Dealer, and on occasions a Mr Friendly, always think of the Maybe You Cannot Afford It Close. It's an almost certain way of doubling your income on that sale.

PSYCHO-CLOSE SEVEN

The Invented Deadline Close

The Invented Deadline Close does not necessarily have to be invented. There will often be times when you have a limited number of end-of-range products, or when you are offering a discount on a service because your company is going through a particularly quiet patch. But if there is no deadline, you can always invent one.

The insurance industry is fortunate in this respect. Frequent changes in taxation and legislation, and anticipated changes prior to the announcement of annual Budget strategies or local or national government elections, give financial services salespeople countless opportunities to present prospects or clients with deadlines that could provide opportunities to save, or make, money if they act quickly.

Creating your own deadlines is a different proposition. You need to be creative and shrewd. You must, of course, also be cautious – unless your artificial deadline appears to be totally genuine you may be found out and as a result lose what might have been a very valuable customer or client.

Suppose you work for a computer software company and sell data-analysis programmes. Your presentation and close could go something along these lines:

> Mr Prospect, we currently have a programme which is being used by some of the major corporations in the country. These have been installed only quite recently and, according to our information, these will be satisfactory for these very large companies until well into the next century. However, we are hiring a team of programmers to develop a new system for us which, frankly, I do not believe is a good decision by our chairman. The costs of this new programme are likely to be at least double that of our existing version. We have a limited supply available of this programme and if you are only looking for something to last you for about twelve years, this is an ideal opportunity for you to buy.

If you are an automobile salesman, you may like to try the following approach:

> Mr Prospect, I have inside information from the sales department at the manufacturers that this model is soon to be replaced by the updated version, which is going to cost some £1000 more. I also happen to know that the increased cost is not justified as the improvements are very minor. However, we will be committed to taking this stock, as will all other dealers, and we are therefore prepared to offer you one of what we believe to be the last few of this model at a discount of 5 per cent (your normal discount anyway).

This type of close is nothing more than a sophisticated version of 'The Last One' close used by so many retailers. Probably the classic example of this is when a customer is being sold a very expensive dress or coat in a store. If she is showing more than the slightest interest the salesperson, if she is a Psycho-Salesperson, will probably say: 'Before you get too enthusiastic about this particular style, I had better check in the storeroom and see if we have your size. This is a very limited edition and has been very popular.' Of course, she returns a few minutes later with the information that there is only one left. The customer always buys it.

Use your imagination and creativity and make your own deadlines. Information from your suppliers, service department or any other pertinent source will help you to create them – and will also help increase your own sales.

PSYCHO-CLOSE EIGHT

The One-Off Opportunity Close

This close can be used to bring forward a potential sale that might not otherwise have happened until some time in the future. It tends to be used mainly for one-off situations like one that involved one of my colleagues on the training circuit.

My colleague was booked to lecture to three groups of salespeople in San Francisco. The flight from London (first class, of course) was forward-booked and was at the height of the season. Another San Francisco company was considering using him for training sessions with their employees. By offering to reduce the cost of his air fares and share them between both clients provided the second company booked him for a particular date, he was able to close the sale immediately.

There may be opportunities for you to share costs between customers or clients at some time, be they your own travel fares, shipping costs or as a result of any other economies of scale that can be achieved through multiple orders.

PSYCHO-CLOSE NINE

The Think It Over Close

Has anybody ever said to you, 'I'll think it over'? If not, you haven't been in sales very long. This has to be every buyer's favourite stall and if you cannot get over it quickly and easily you will be at the mercy of every prospect you come across.

By using the Think It Over Close you will welcome that stall with open arms and know that you have the ability to close the sale there and then. The only person who will be thinking anything over will be you – thinking over and over again about what you are going to do with your big, fat commission cheque.

The salesman in the following role play has done a very good job in presenting to his prospect. He has tried several closes yet, in spite of his efforts:

> **Prospect:** I'll think it over, thank you.
>
> **Salesman:** *I'm sure that's a very sensible idea Mr Prospect. Having gone into all the benefits of this product in such detail and seeing how they can assist you in improving your office administration, can I assume that you will be giving this very, very careful consideration?*
>
> **Prospect** (now he thinks he is really off the hook): Yes, of course I will.
>
> **Salesman:** *I am pleased to hear that Mr Prospect. Just to satisfy myself, you wouldn't be saying this just to get rid of me, would you?*
>
> **Prospect:** No, of course not. Everything you have told me so far is very interesting and will most certainly be of benefit to our company.
>
> **Salesman:** *I am very pleased to hear that Mr Prospect. Just as a matter of interest, and before I go, could you tell me precisely what it is that you will be thinking over – is it the money?*
>
> (There is absolutely no pause between thinking it over and 'is it the money?').

The prospect is now completely on the spot again. He has to admit that it is the money, or he has to come up with a very valid objection that has not been raised before or that has been raised before and which you have failed to satisfy. The latter should not be the case.

The Think It Over Close is just another way of finding the real objection. Its power for Psycho-Salespeople is based on the fact that because the prospect believes you are going he finally opens up. If he raises a final objection I am sure you will have no problem in finding a final solution.

Another, very clever, version of this close follows.

PSYCHO-CLOSE TEN

The Door Knob Close

The Door Knob Close can be used successfully with all psychological types but particularly with conceptual buyers. If the hidden objection is factual the close will work equally well with analytical ones.

It relies on two factors. The first is that, as with the Think It Over

Close, the prospect believes he or she is completely off the hook. The second is the sympathy factor.

When you have completely given up on the sale and it is unlikely that you will have the opportunity to return and make your presentation again, you pack your briefcase, rise from your chair and thank your prospect warmly for seeing you and giving you the opportunity to demonstrate your product or service to them. As you get to the door, you turn around and make the following statement:

Mr Prospect, I hope you don't mind me asking but, as I am sure you are aware, I make my living selling this particular product. I thought I had presented it to you properly. I felt you had the need for it and that I had demonstrated the benefits to you accurately. I was quite certain that you would want to buy it. Just so that I don't make the same mistake again, could you please tell me where I went wrong?

Your prospect thinks he is off the hook. He is sympathetic and eager to help. He finally gives you the real reason. If you are not back in the chair in front of him in less than fifteen seconds, I will be amazed. If you have not closed the sale within the next ten minutes, you should also be amazed.

This close and many other similar closes depend a great deal upon your acting ability. However, as I have already said, when you are selling you are on stage – and you had better be a good actor.

PSYCHO-CLOSE ELEVEN

The Assumptive, or Secondary Question, Close

Use this close when you are fairly certain that your prospect is willing to accept your proposition and all that is necessary is to put it to bed quickly. The technique is based on posing the major buying question first, then immediately bypassing it with a secondary question of lesser importance.

For example, in the case of our automobile salesman, the closing question would go like this:

Salesman: *I think we have covered everything now Mr Prospect. We just need to complete the order form. By the way, will you be arranging your own insurance, or would you like us to arrange this for you?*

Prospect: I will be arranging my own insurance, thank you. [They've bought it.]

A computer salesman:
Salesman: *From what we have discussed so far Mr Prospect, I think the 210 megabyte model is going to be most suitable for you. Would you prefer it with one floppy drive or two?*
Prospect: I think one would suit our needs. [They've bought it.]

A travel agent:
Salesperson: *The Bahamas seems to be the ideal holiday for you and your family. Will you be paying by cheque or credit card?*
Prospect: By credit card. [They've bought it.]

The psychology behind this type of close is very simple. As I said earlier, it is the salesperson's responsibility to make the close as easy and painless for the prospect as possible. Giving him or her the opportunity to agree to some very minor point means that the major decision, and the most expensive one, is taken out of the picture completely.

Buyer resistance vanishes with the Secondary Question Close.

PSYCHO-CLOSE TWELVE

The Satisfied Centre of Influence Close

Almost every salesperson has one particularly important client whom they go out of their way to satisfy no matter what the cost. He or she is particularly well looked after because of the volumes of business they place, their many contacts and the fact that their name is instantly recognizable when used as a reference.

Developing a relationship with this particular centre of influence can be a tremendous help in closing the occasional very large sale, provided, of course, that you do not take advantage of it too often.

First, obtain his or her permission to use them occasionally as a reference for you and your product or service. Ask if they would be prepared, on the odd occasion, to accept a telephone call from a prospective customer or client seeking a reference. Also ask them whether they would occasionally be prepared to join you for breakfast or lunch if a prospect was particularly important to you.

Provided you are delivering a lot more than would normally be expected of you, this permission will certainly be granted. It will reap valuable rewards for you many times over in the future.

If you have several such customers or clients, all the better. Try and obtain written references from each and every one of them. Have them laminated between two sheets of plastic to keep them in perfect condition and take them with you wherever you go. Nothing speaks more strongly than a third-party reference.

PSYCHO-CLOSE THIRTEEN

The Weak Spot Close

Some years ago I was involved with a house-building company in Scotland. We had built a number of small, luxury, holiday homes on a lakeshore site. They had the most magnificent views but, because of cost constraints, the rooms had been kept to a minimal size and we had not been able to use the highest standards of fixtures and fittings as we would have wished. Nevertheless, the homes were selling reasonably well although not nearly as fast as we had hoped.

One bright afternoon I was showing a prospective purchaser and his wife around the development and was keen to sell the house in which they had expressed some slight interest. It was one of the first to be built and had been on our hands a long time.

The very first thing my prospect's wife said when she walked into the kitchen was: 'Oh, what a wonderful view. I was brought up in a home overlooking a lake and I have always wanted to live somewhere like this again.' This was her weak spot and my hot button. We then moved into the living-room. The husband expressed concern at its dimensions. I immediately pointed out the open fireplace and the wonderful view across the lake. We then moved upstairs into the first bedroom. The same sequence of events took place there and in the other two bedrooms. In each case the husband expressed concern at the size of the rooms and also commented on the quality of the fixtures and fittings. I agreed, and pointed out the wonderful view across the lake from each bedroom.

Although I was talking to the husband all the time, I was really selling to the wife. It came as no surprise to me that, after a few minutes by themselves in their car, they returned and made me an offer. I refused this and stuck out for the full asking price. 'Is there anywhere else with a view across a lake quite like this?' I asked. They bought the house at the full market price.

Identify weak spots. They occur in almost every type of market and with almost every type of buyer. Whenever an objection is raised, answer it and then remind your prospect of the single feature that is so attractive to them.

PSYCHO-CLOSE FOURTEEN

The Take It Home and Try It Close

This one almost never fails. It can only be used for products – ideally, luxury ones. Provided you have a reasonable supply of a particular item, and if your prospect just cannot be closed on the sale, let him or her take it home and use it for a few days.

I know of one company who started doing this with second-hand cars when the fashion for having two cars in a family first started.

Imagine the scene. Our prospect's wife is lent a shiny second-hand car. She gets to use it, the neighbours get to see it, the children get to ride around in it and our prospect's friends get to know about it. Can he really give it back? Can he really lose face with his neighbours, his friends and his children? Could he ever tell his wife that it is going back again?

If a product is expensive and you stand to make a good profit on selling it, let your prospect use it. The cost to you of the rare damaged return will be far outweighed by the money you earn on products that never come back. If you have got it and can spare it – lend it.

PSYCHO-CLOSE FIFTEEN

The Blank Order Form Close

Almost every product or service requires an order form or authority for your prospect to sign. If you do not have one, design one.

Without making it too obvious, try and make sure that your order form is in front of you and in view of your prospect either at the start of your presentation or some time during it when you produce reference literature or testimonials. At some stage, when you feel your prospect is ready to be closed, ask for a piece of information that you require in order to fulfil their order and write it on the form. It could be your prospect's full name, their company's name or address or information relating to one of the products or services you are selling.

The moment your prospect sees you write something on your blank order form and does not question it, you know they have bought. The rest of the sale is a mere formality.

In some sales situations it can be appropriate to enter the company's name and address on the form even before you get into the meeting. By leaving this in full view of your prospect, with his or her name and address at the top in bold capital letters, you are sending a very clear message to their subconscious mind that you expect a sale. If you can do this and get away with it, you are almost half-way there before you have started.

PSYCHO-CLOSE SIXTEEN

The Oliver Twist Close

Whenever you sell a product that is sold in quantity, or if it is part of a range of products, don't forget the Oliver Twist Close – ask them to buy more!

Every Psycho-Salesperson knows that the best time to sell is when they have just sold something. They are on a high, in a selling mode. They are enthusiastic because of their success and cannot wait to get to the next appointment and do it all over again. Why not do it with the same customer?

Many salespeople forget that just as they can be in a selling mode, a buyer who has just bought is almost invariably in a buying mode. With both of you in your respective frames of mind you could very easily double, treble or quadruple the volume or range of products you sell.

There could be some very straightforward and financial benefit to the buyer in buying more: extra discounts for volume purchases, extra support material or other incentives provided by your company or yourself.

Surely you can convince your customer that by stocking the whole range, instead of part of it, he or she could more than double their sales and their income. Never forget that when someone has just bought from you their defences are at their lowest. This is your unique opportunity to double your income.

With so many exciting Psycho-Closes at your fingertips, how can you possibly fail to double your income? Your subconscious is already totally convinced. Closing the sale after a good presentation has never been difficult. Using these techniques it will be even easier.

PSYCHO-DYNAMIC EXERCISES

There is one more lesson that you need to learn this week and it is so important that, once again, we are going to use Psycho-Dynamic Programming to get it into your subconscious once and for all.

Earlier we discussed the fact that many salespeople fail to ask for an order. I also showed that the vast majority never attempt to close more than twice before quitting. This must never happen to you.

From now on you will never leave a prospect without attempting to close the sale – and attempting to close it in at least five different ways and at five different times during your presentation. In addition, you will never, ever, leave your prospect without asking for the names of at least three other people they know who they believe your product or service might be suitable for. This applies whether or not you have sold to the prospect. At the end of your evening relaxation exercise, therefore, after you have spent ten minutes concentrating on your power word associations, you will spend a further ten minutes repeating over and over the following statement:

> *Every time I make a presentation to a prospect, I will do my very best to close the sale. I will make at least five closing attempts. Five closing attempts is the absolute minimum. At the end of every sales presentation I will ask for at least three referred leads and I will obtain them.*

This week should be your very best week yet. You have almost all the tools you are going to need to increase your sales beyond your wildest dreams. Go out and use them.

Summary of Key Points

● Many salespeople fail to attempt to close.

● The average salesperson attempts only two closes.

● Psycho-Salespeople attempt at least five closes if necessary.

● Learn and practise the sixteen Psycho-Closes in this chapter.

● After your evening exercises, repeat over and over again for ten minutes: *'Every time I make a presentation to a prospect, I will do my very best to close the sale. I will make at least five closing attempts. Five closing attempts is the absolute minimum. At the end of every sales presentation I will ask for at least three referred leads and I will obtain them.'*

● *Enter your sales figures for the week.*

WEEK EIGHT

YOU HAVE
THE POWER!

WHO DO YOU WORK FOR?

At a recent training seminar for a group of over 150 salespeople from
various companies I opened the first session with the request: 'Please
put your hand up if you are your own boss.' Thirty-five hands were
raised. I then asked who were employees. The remaining hands shot
up. By the end of the weekend, every person attending the seminar
had come to the inescapable conclusion that they worked for nobody
but themselves. They were the boss. The buck stopped with them.

Anybody who is remunerated, either partially or completely, on a
results basis has to come to terms with the fact that they work for themselves, and that only they can be responsible for their success.

THE COURAGE IT TAKES

No matter how well you have been taught, and no matter how much
you have learnt, you will have been wasting your time if you don't
have the power, courage and determination to take action. I will give
you all three.

Seven years ago a close friend of mine was very badly burned in a
boating accident. A fault on the outboard motor ignited the petrol line
and caused an explosion in the fuel tanks. He was taken to hospital
suffering from first-degree burns and was given only hours to live.

After months and months of painful treatment, dozens of operations for skin grafts and several other operations which managed to save the sight in one of his eyes, he emerged from hospital in a wheelchair.

During his period of convalescence his business failed, he lost his home and most of his savings were used up. He was told he would never get out of a wheelchair again. Fortunately, he had the courage and determination to fight on.

Today he walks with a slight limp, is the chairman of his own very successful publishing company and has bought back the family home he had lost some years ago.

Do you recognize the following person from this brief biography?

He lost his business at age 31.
He was defeated in a legislative race at 32.
He failed again in business at age 34.
His childhood sweetheart died when he was 35 years old.
He had a nervous breakdown at 36 years of age.
He lost a state election at age 38.
He lost a congressional race at age 43, another at age 46
   and yet another at age 48.
He failed to become a state senator when he was 55.
He failed to become elected vice-president at age 56.
He lost another senatorial race at age 58.
He was elected President of the United States of America
   at age 60.

His name was Abraham Lincoln.

There comes a time in everyone's life when they face the ultimate challenge. They have to make a decision to give up or to harness every ounce of power, courage and determination and fight for what they want. In my friend's case, it was for his life. In your case, it is for the life you want to lead.

You too will need those qualities to carry on fighting for what you know can be yours, irrespective of the trials and tribulations you may have to go through to achieve your objectives.

THE POWER WITHIN YOU

A great many of the techniques which culminated in Psycho-Dynamic Programming come from the study of ancient religions and tribal ceremonies. Using modern scientific instruments and other research facilities we have been able to tap into the techniques of mind control that have enabled man to walk on fire, sleep on beds of nails, lift weights many times heavier than his own body and cast voodoo spells – techniques that have also been responsible for many other seemingly supernatural phenomena that have been recorded over the centuries.

Try this simple experiment. Sit comfortably in a chair and, holding your hands outstretched, place your palms as close together as you can without actually touching. You feel heat.

Now move your hands a little more apart. Feel the heat again. Now move them slightly more apart. If at any time you fail to feel the heat, move your hands a little closer together until the sensation reappears. Now move your hands until they are approximately 10–12 centimetres (4–5 inches) apart. You still feel it. Try moving them even wider and wider apart. With a little practice you should be able to feel a strong sensation between the palms of your hands even when they are 45–60 centimetres (1½–2 feet) apart or more. Everyone can do this with just a little practice.

Heat cannot possibly transmit itself over this distance. This is not heat, this is power!

The sensation you can feel and mould between your hands when they are 60–90 centimetres (2–3 feet) apart is powerful life energy. Your whole body, and the whole universe, is filled with it. This energy is yours and yours to be used. What you choose to do with it during the course of your last week is for you to decide. What you choose to do with it for the rest of your life is also for you to decide. It is a natural law that the more you use this power, the faster it is replenished. You can never use it up; you can channel it and make the very best use of it or you can allow it to dissipate slowly and be wasted.

As a Psycho-Salesperson you need only know that it is there and that you can draw on it constantly and at any time you wish. You have the power.

BELIEVE AND ACT

One person who believes they can do something is worth eighty who believe they cannot. I have mentioned statistics which prove that in most sales forces over 80 per cent of the business produced is done by less than 20 per cent of the salespeople. In most cases, salesmen and saleswomen have not had the opportunity to benefit from Psycho-Dynamic sales training, and have had little to rely upon other than themselves. The fact is that they believed they could do it, they did it and they carried on doing it. You have the benefit of having learnt some of the very best ingredients of Psycho-Selling. You know how to prospect, how to present yourself and your product, how to analyse and make use of your buyers' very different psychological types and how to close the sale.

You have all the tools you need. All you have to do is believe this and hold this belief constantly in your mind.

Acting as if you have already achieved what you set out to do is one of the most powerful Psycho-Dynamic Programming exercises you can ever carry out. If, after seven weeks, you are still driving the same car but know you are working your way to owning the one currently pictured in your scrap-book, pretend you are driving the car of your dreams. At traffic lights sit upright and proud. Believe that people are looking at you and admiring you and the car you are driving. You are the epitome of success. When you walk into your prospect's reception room and introduce yourself to the receptionist stand tall, stand proud and give your name as if you were announcing the most confident, most successful and most wealthy salesperson in your field. When you take your wife or husband out to dinner at the end of a hard and successful week's work, walk through the restaurant tall and erect and proud. You will notice that people notice you as they have never noticed you before.

Posture, stance, the set of your chin and the expression on your face have significant impact on the various chemical systems within your body that make you feel the way you do. If you walk with your head down and your shoulders hunched the chemical changes that take place affect your brain cells and their sensory mechanisms making you feel low and depressed. Standing tall and erect with your shoulders back, your stomach in and your head tilted slightly backwards has the opposite effect. It tells your brain to tell you that you are positive, proud, courageous, determined and have the power to achieve what you have set out to do.

Power Gestures

Throughout this book you will have come across power phrases that you can use to reinforce your presentations. What about power gestures?

Next time you are watching the news on television or reading a newspaper and see a film or photograph of a powerful political or business leader, study that person. If you go to the theatre or cinema, study the actor or comedian who has the audience spellbound. What are they doing? Look at the way they hold their heads. Look at the expression on their faces and the way they use gestures to illustrate or reinforce a particular point. These people hold massive audiences in the palms of their hands because of the way they express themselves, because of their gestures and tone of voice and the way they speak.

If you have a video recording machine, tape a scene or speech on television that has a particular impact on you. Play it again, over and over. The expressions and gestures that had such an impact on you and your sensory system had the same effect on hundreds of thousands of other people. Make these expressions and gestures your own, build them into your sales presentations and closing interviews and you will capture the power that has taken the people you imitate to the very pinnacle of success.

POWER WHENEVER YOU NEED IT

The following technique will enable you to harness the greatest amount of power, confidence and energy whenever you most need it. I have taught it to thousands of people and many claim it was the ultimate key to their success.

I want you to stand up proud and erect, with your right arm held out in front of you and with your palm facing upwards. I now want you to think back to the most successful episode in your life that you can remember. It may have been the time you won the 100-metre sprint at your school. If that is the case, you should remember how you felt, how your body tingled with excitement and how proud you were. You should be able to hear the crowd cheering and feel your chest swelling with pride. You must feel all those wonderful sensations coursing through you again.

It may be the occasion when you put on your very best sales present-ation and closed the very best sale of your life so far. If that is the case, remember how you felt when you left your customer's office. Remem-ber the feeling of power, pride, exhilaration and excitement.

Whatever the occasion that made you feel so wonderful, bring back every memory of it as vividly as you can. Then imagine those memo-ries and feelings sitting in the palm of your right hand. At the very height of the experience, when you feel at your most powerful, close your fingers over these feelings, clench your fist and say quietly and very powerfully, 'Yes!'

From now on, whenever you need to be at your very best, and if ever you lack the confidence or determination to do what you know has to be done, you need only clench your fist and quietly and forcefully say, 'Yes!'. All the power, courage and determination you need will be yours.

As your sales get bigger and bigger and your success gets better and better, you will have many more experiences that create the same feel-ings of power and exhilaration. Don't waste them. In a quiet moment, as soon as possible after that incident, pour those feelings into your open right hand and wrap your fingers around them. At the end of just a few weeks the power of your clenched fist will become ever greater, leading you on to achievements you never dreamed were possible.

THE 100th MONKEY

Are you a sales manager or sales director in charge of a large group of people? If so, the story of the 100th monkey may be of considerable interest to you.

Some years ago a group of American scientists studied the behaviour of wild monkeys that inhabited several very small Polynesian islands. The monkeys had virtually no contact with humans and lived on a diet that consisted almost entirely of bananas and other wild fruits.

The scientists decided to introduce a new type of food to the monkeys and selected sweet potatoes for the experiment. These were dumped by the sackful on the beaches of each island. The potatoes were covered in particles of sand and their gritty taste had no appeal for the monkeys and for some weeks they were almost ignored.

One day a baby monkey accidentally rolled one of the sweet potatoes into the sea and pulled it out again. The water had washed the particles of sand from the skin and, for the first time, a monkey enjoyed a sweet potato. Several of his playmates started to copy him and very soon several monkeys were sitting on the beach enjoying their first taste of this new food.

A few days later up to eighty or ninety monkeys were on the beach in the morning, enjoying their sweet potatoes. Then something almost miraculous happened. At around the time that the 100th monkey on the island washed and ate a sweet potato, all the other monkeys on every other island who had previously rejected this food came almost simultaneously to the beaches and started washing the sweet potatoes in the sea and eating them.

Nobody had shown them what to do but, for reasons we still do not understand, this consciousness suddenly spread throughout the entire monkey population and a new way of life began.

We still do not know the mechanism that makes a change of consciousness almost automatic throughout a population. However, the moral to this story is that when enough of your salespeople are doing the right thing it is likely that a primitive instinct deep within the subconscious will be alerted and many more of them will start to achieve the success your company needs, and that they can enjoy. It is your responsibility to find the 100th monkey.

WHAT DO YOU DO THIS WEEK?

What you do this week is up to you. You now have all the tools you will ever need to become the very best salesperson in the world. You also have a choice. Do you want to be? The rest is up to you.

However, I would like you to do one further thing. Once again, as in an earlier chapter, I want you to buy a small quantity of self-adhesive labels. This time, I want you to write the following words on each one:

I can, I want to, I will!

Stick the labels on your bathroom mirror, the dashboard of your car, your diary, your desk and your telephone. Put them where you will come across them constantly throughout the day.

Every time you see one of these labels, clench your fist and say quietly and with power, 'Yes!'. And, with all the courage and power available to you, go out there this week and prospect, present and close those sales!

Summary of Key Points

● Anyone who is remunerated on a results basis is their own boss. Nobody else is responsible for their success.

● No matter what you are taught, you need the power, courage and determination to put your lessons into action.

● You have the power to do whatever you want. Use your Psycho-Dynamic programming exercises to harness it.

● Act as if you have already achieved everything you want to achieve.

● Study the voices, facial expressions and gestures of great achievers and make these a part of you.

● If you are a sales manager, find your 100th monkey.

● Make up labels carrying the message 'I can, I want to, I will!' Whenever you see them, use the clenched-fist power programme.

● Carry out your morning and evening exercises.

● Have your best sales week ever and record your results.

SUMMARY

Most salespeople are in a hurry. We want results and we want them fast. Contained within these pages is everything you need to make them happen fast.

I know that some of you will have flicked through the book, picked out some of the very best tips for prospecting, presenting and closing your sales and chosen to carry out just a few of the exercises that have appealed to you most.

I am almost certain that you will nevertheless be well on your way to doubling your income or will already have doubled it.

If you are one of these people I urge you to go back to the beginning, start again and do it properly.

There are no substitutes for experience and you will never know the power of Psycho-Dynamic Programming until you have experienced it for yourself.

Those of you who have followed this eight-week programme religiously will know, and have, the power. Thinking back over what you have achieved since starting the programme should make you want to carry on. Continue doing your morning and evening relaxation exercises and repeat the visualization ones you found most useful every day for the rest of your selling career. Re-read this book frequently so that you never forget the brilliant techniques you have learned for prospecting, presenting and closing the sale.

APPENDIX
RECORD KEEPING

Week No	A	B	C	D
1				
2				
3				
4				
5				
6				
7				
8				

In Column A enter the best eight-consecutive-weeks sales figures you have achieved in the last twelve months and in Column B write the income you earned as a result of these sales. At the end of each week of your course in Psycho-Selling enter your sales figures in Column C and the income achieved from these in Column D.

Other business titles published by BBC Books:

Doing Business in Japan by Jonathan Rice
Trouble Shooter by John Harvey-Jones and Anthea Masey
Trouble Shooter 2 by John Harvey-Jones
The Adventurers by Anthea Masey
How Do You Manage? by John Nicholson
Inside Organisations by Charles Handy
Women and Power by Nancy Kline